Da Capo Press Music Reprint Series
GENERAL EDITOR
FREDERICK FREEDMAN
VASSAR COLLEGE

KEYBOARD MUSIC
FROM THE MIDDLE AGES
TO THE BEGINNINGS OF THE BAROQUE

NIMBED POPE PLAYING A POSITIVE ORGAN SURROUNDED
BY A CARDINAL AND TWO BISHOPS (POSSIBLY S. GREGORY,
S. JEROME (BELLOWS) AND SS. AMBROSE AND AUGUSTINE)

Late 15th century French or Flemish

KEYBOARD MUSIC
FROM THE MIDDLE AGES

TO THE BEGINNINGS OF THE BAROQUE

By Gerald Stares Bedbrook

New Preface by the Author
New Introduction by F.E. Kirby

DA CAPO PRESS • NEW YORK • 1973

Library of Congress Cataloging in Publication Data

Bedbrook, Gerald Stares.
   Keyboard music from the Middle Ages to the
beginnings of the Baroque.

  (Da Capo Press music reprint series)
  "An unabridged and slightly corrected republication
of the first edition published in London in 1949."
  Bibliography: p.
  1. Harpsichord music—History and criticism.
2. Organ music—History and criticism. I. Title.
ML549.B4   1973   786'.09   69-15605
ISBN 0-306-71056-0

This Da Capo Press edition of *Keyboard Music from the Middle Ages to the Beginnings of the Baroque* is an unabridged and slightly corrected republication of the first edition published in London in 1949. It is reprinted by special arrangement with Macmillan & Company Limited, London.

The following new material has been prepared for this edition: a new preface by the author; a new introduction by F.E. Kirby; and a new bibliography compiled by the author and Professor Kirby, and edited by Frederick Freedman.

To

MARGARET E. BROADBRIDGE

INTRODUCTION

A nyone who delves into the history of music becomes immediately aware—all too often painfully so—that much of
the most important material—encyclopedias, bibliographical
works, general histories, specialized monographs, critical editions, and the like—is available only in some foreign language
or other, usually German. This situation has prevailed to a
much greater extent in the past, but we are nonetheless still
confronted with it. In 1949, when Gerald Stares Bedbrook first
brought out his *Keyboard Music from the Middle Ages to the
Beginnings of the Baroque,* the two standard works dealing
with the history of keyboard music were Seiffert's on harpsichord music and Frotscher's on organ music, both in German,
and both containing, although by no means limited to, extensive
discussions of the keyboard music of the middle ages, the renaissance, and the early baroque; in French, there was Rokseth's
extensive treatment of late medieval-early renaissance organ
music.[1] There also existed, in German, a comprehensive survey
of piano music by Georgii which includes some treatment of
harpsichord music.[2] Even the 1910 dissertation by the man who

[1] Max Seiffert, *Geschichte der Klaviermusik* (Leipzig: Breitkopf & Härtel,
1899; reprint, Hildesheim: G. Olms, 1966) and Gotthold Frotscher, *Geschichte
des Orgelspiels und der Orgelkomposition,* 2 vols. (Berlin-Schöneberg: M. Hesse,
1928–36; reprint, Berlin: Merseburger, 1959). Incidentally, both of these are
reworkings of earlier books: Seiffert's goes back to Carl Friedrich Weitzmann,
Geschichte des Clavierspiels und der Clavierliteratur (Stuttgart: J. G. Cotta,
1863), which was, rather exceptionally, translated into English by Theodore
Baker as *A History of Pianoforte-Playing and Pianoforte Literature* (New York:
G. Schirmer, 1897; reprint, New York: Da Capo Press, 1969): while Frotscher's
goes back to August Gottfried Ritter, *Zur Geschichte des Orgelspiels, vornehmlich
des Deutschen, im 14. bis zum Anfang des 19. Jahrhunderts,* 2 vols. (Leipzig: M.
Hesse, 1884). Yvonne Rokseth, *La musique d'orgue an XVe siècle et au début
de XVIe* (Paris: Librairie Droz, 1930).
[2] Walter Georgii, *Klaviermusik* (Zurich: Atlantis, 1941; 4th ed., 1965).

was to become the dean of American musicology, Otto Kinkeldey, which deals with keyboard instruments and keyboard music
in the sixteenth century, was available only in German.[3]

At the end of World War II, the relatively few books available in the English language concerned with the history of keyboard music were of a more or less popular nature. As principal
examples we may mention those by Bie (the translation of a
German book), Krehbiel, Westerby, Wier, and Hutcheson.[4]
These works may generally be described as guides for players
of piano music that point out typical examples of late renaissance keyboard music in the hope of bringing an element of
variety into performers' repertory. A truly scholarly history of
keyboard music in English, to say nothing of a book dealing
specifically with early keyboard music, was completely lacking,
and indeed the prospect of such a work seemed at the time
highly improbable, although competent studies of individual
composers and musical forms did exist.

Since that time, however, the picture has changed radically.
In 1947, as a herald of the coming change, there appeared Willi
Apel's outline of the history of keyboard music.[5] This book,
among the first of its prolific author's many and important contributions to the study in this country of music history, was the
first comprehensive scholarly survey of early keyboard music to
appear in English. Kenyon's discussion of the harpsichord and
harpsichord music was published two years later,[6] and was fol-

[3] Otto Kinkeldey, *Orgel und Klavier in der Musik des 16. Jahrunderts* (Leipzig: Breitkopf & Härtel, 1910; reprint, Hildesheim: G. Olms, 1968).

[4] Oskar Bie, *A History of the Pianoforte and Pianoforte Players,* trans. & rev. by E. E. Kellett and E. W. Naylor (London: J. E. Dent, 1899; reprint, with a fore-ward by Abe Tzerko, New York: Da Capo Press, 1966), the translation of *Das Klavier und seine Meister* (Munich: F. Bruckmann, 1898); Henry E. Krehbiel, *The Pianoforte and its Music* (New York: Scribners, 1911); Herbert Westerby, *A History of Pianoforte Music* (London: Kegan Paul, Trench, Trubner & Co., 1924; reprint, New York: Da Capo Press, 1971); Albert E. Wier, *The Piano: Its History, Makers, Players and Music* (New York: Longmans, Green & Co., 1940) and Ernest Hutcheson, *The Literature of the Piano* (New York: A. A. Knopf, 1948; 3rd ed., revised by Rudolph Ganz, New York: A. A. Knopf, 1964).

[5] Willi Apel, *Masters of the Keyboard* (Cambridge: Harvard University Press, 1947).

[6] Max Kenyon, *Harpsichord Music: A Survey of the Virginals, Spinet and Harp-sichord* (London: Cassell, 1949).

lowed in 1954 by Friskin and Freundlich's comprehensive survey of the entire repertory of piano music, including a good deal of harpsichord music.[7]

When Bedbrook's book appeared in 1949, it quite literally broke new ground. Where else in English at the time could one have found comparable discussions of the Robertsbridge Manuscript, of the German manuscript collections of the fifteenth century, of Andrea and Giovanni Gabrieli, of Claudio Merulo, of Frescobaldi? One must remember that neither Gustave Reese's indispensable guide to renaissance music nor the corresponding volume of the *New Oxford History of Music* had yet appeared, and that publication of the comprehensive German encyclopedia *Die Musik in Geschichte und Gegenwart* was barely underway.

For the most part, Bedbrook organizes the subject chronologically. The book is divided into three parts: the first on the middle ages, the second on the renaissance, and the third on the "north European schools and the beginnings of the baroque." He begins his account with a brief survey of the organ and organ music in the middle ages and then settles down to the fourteenth and fifteenth centuries, presenting a good deal of material on the German organ music of the fifteenth century. He evidently viewed the renaissance as a primarily Italian phenomenon, since German, French, and English keyboard music up to 1600 is all discussed under the section dealing with the medieval period; the Spaniard Cabezón, however, is treated under the renaissance. Close to one third of the book is devoted to a discussion of the Italian keyboard music of the sixteenth century. The historical presentation draws to an end with sections given over largely to accounts of Sweelinck and Frescobaldi. Here and there Bedbrook gives descriptions of the instruments themselves, concentrating particularly on early forms of the organ, and, in a concluding chapter, he provides an important treatment of keyboard technique in the sixteenth century, notably dealing

---

[7] James Friskin and Irwin Freundlich, *Music for the Piano: A Handbook of Concert and Teaching Material from 1580 to 1952* (New York: Rinehart & Co., 1954; reprint, New York: Da Capo Press, 1971).

with the system of fingering that prevailed at that time, as explained in Diruta's *Il transilvano* (1597). Finally, the value of the book is greatly enhanced by the inclusion of numerous music examples, lavish and carefully selected illustrations, and an extensive topically organized bibliography which even contains a list of phonograph recordings.

It is to be expected that a book of this kind, appearing when it did, would suffer some defects. Perhaps the most important of these is the frequent inclusion of extensive discussions of repertories that are not properly keyboard music. Bedbrook seems to have assumed, along with a great many others, that the works of Landino and Machaut were intended largely for organ, whereas in fact they are polyphonic ensemble compositions for voices and instruments in whose performance the organ, in one form or other, could well have participated. Although transcriptions (intabulations or intavolaturas) of such works for keyboard were made in the fourteenth and fifteenth centuries, the fact remains that originally these compositions were written for a different medium of performance. Furthermore, many of the works of Adrian Willaert, Jacques Buus, Annibale Padovano and the Gabrielis that are taken up are not strictly keyboard compositions, but were rather intended for performance by either an instrumental ensemble or keyboard. Also, while Bedbrook makes the point that the leading polyphonic forms of the thirteenth century are not organ music, his inclusion of such a relatively detailed discussion of them in this book may have placed upon them a misleading emphasis. On the other hand, an important source like the Faenza Manuscript—the largest source of keyboard music from the fourteenth century—is omitted: it was scarcely known at the time.

It is, however, greatly to Bedbrook's credit that the material is presented with an affirmative attitude. Instead of regarding early keyboard compositions as primitive feeble attempts which eventually evolved and produced the efflorescence of the baroque, as was so often the attitude of that time, Bedbrook discusses the music sympathetically, indeed enthusiastically, on its own terms in the evident hope of persuading the reader to continue explorations on his own. As he says in the Preface (p. xxii): "This music of the past, including that of the middle ages, is not properly regarded as archaic or experimental, but must be considered as no less perfect in its own way than that of later musicians." This attitude informs his entire presentation.

Conditions have changed a good deal since 1949. The celebrated explosion of knowledge has affected the history of music in general and the history of keyboard music in particular. In a way, Bedbrook's book stands as a symbol of things to come, yet, to some extent, it also stands as a victim of the progress it anticipated, and in several ways it has been superseded as more material has been made widely available. But such is the fate of all works of scholarship. Among more recent studies that deal in some detail with the keyboard music of the middle ages and the renaissance we may cite those by Young, Gillespie, and Kirby;[8] and just recently published we have the monumental book by Apel, the result of decades of work, treating at great length and in meticulous detail the history of keyboard music up to 1700—in German.[9] Also, a considerable amount of the early keyboard music itself has been published since 1949, so that much of the music Bedbrook discusses is now readily available. The most grandiose project in this field is the *Corpus of Early Keyboard Music,* under the editorship (again!) of Willi Apel, devoted to keyboard music composed up to and including the seventeenth century. Nevertheless, Bedbrook's pioneering book may well be said to have played an important part in this development, and it is good to have it in circulation once more.

As a partial updating of Bedbrook's bibliography, the reader is referred to the comprehensive bibliographies in Young, Gil-

[8] William Young, "Keyboard Music to 1600," *Musica Disciplina* XVI (1962), 115–50 and XVII (1963), 163–93; John Gillespie, *Five Centuries of Keyboard Music* (Belmont, Calif.: Wadsworth, 1965); F. E. Kirby, *A Short History of Keyboard Music* (New York: Free Press, 1966).

[9] Willi Apel, *Geschichte der Orgel- und Klaviermusik bis 1700* (Kassel: Bärenreiter, 1967). Subsequent to the completion of this Introduction an English edition of this work was published as: *The History of Keyboard Music to 1700,* translated and revised by Hans Tischler (Bloomington: Indiana University Press, 1972).

lespie, and Kirby (see note 8) as well as the "New Bibliography" included in this volume.

F. E. Kirby

Lake Forest College
Lake Forest, Illinois

PREFACE TO THE 1973 EDITION

In the days when this book was first submitted to press, the bombs were still dropping on London. Manuscripts abroad were inaccessible, while those at home were put away in safe keeping. Mr. Gerald Cooper kindly lent me his photographs of the Buxheim Book (the only set in England), and I was lucky in getting the Heborgh prints from Philadelphia. A German library efficiently remembered to send photographs ordered before the War, while a Polish one suggested that soap or books could be used in exchange for photostats, after hostilities. Such were the conditions of research at that time. Nevertheless, information poured in, and it was possible through a delayed printing to add to the text. The Faenza 117 photostats came in too late, and I was afterwards made aware of the English contents of the Lynar MSS at Lubbenau.

In those days, Byrd and Bull were still looked upon by the average English musician as the progenitors of most keyboard music. Frescobaldi had a dim recess in the organ loft, while the Gabrielis were only known to the extremely cultivated. Now, Giovanni has become a 'prom night' in this country, while transcripts of the earliest German tablatures can be found in shops and libraries and taken home and played. A welcome advance. It was a pleasure indeed when Finn Viderö first recorded some Sweelinck and Frescobaldi on the Frederiksborg Organ at Denmark. Today, most early instruments have been reconstructed, perhaps not always with authentic fidelity, but at least the effort has been made. All that is left now is to play the music and make a personal assessment.

My original plan was to explore the musical past, discover its nature, and evaluate its aesthetic qualities, believing it impossible that music had no meaning to the people of that time save that of function. Subjective valuation has got into hot water, however, and the statistical examination of the component parts is now considered the only true method of estimation. Statistics, on the other hand, can be as fickle as taste. In the long run, all musical judgement is made from a standard common to all listeners; otherwise there would never have been only one Haydn or Mozart, and every history book would have been different. So, it was by the constant playing of these works that their value was assessed.

Considering that neither rhythmic nor harmonic variety is to be expected at that period, it is amazing how these composers never repeated themselves, each work having a quality of its own. Judging by the snow-deep researches on these early worlds, a traveller from space might imagine this to have been the most popular period in music—unaware that the joy of discovering music can sometimes excel the actual pleasure of listening to it. Yet, no study, however obtuse, has failed to shed some light on this age. No doubt, the modern musician wants to know what makes the music "tick"— what methods were employed. With the increasing awareness of formal structure of the fugue and sonata, the contemporary student has been given the idea that structure can be learnt. Forms had existed in all cultures long before that time, however, and were in essence the outcome of personal expression conditioned by circumstances. Let us see how this happened in early Europe, and in keyboard music in particular.

All music, East and West, was primarily based on a tradition of sacred or secular melodies. The music of Europe was largely dominated by the length of the liturgical text and the various verse forms of the day. Yet, even then, syllables were prolonged by melismas or worked into cadences at the ends of phrases. On the employment of certain decorations upon the sacred chants of Europe, obtained presumably from various local traditions, the problem arose of dealing with another voice or voices. At first, the decorations were more or less at the same pitch level, and there was no idea of part-writing as such. By the twelfth and thirteenth centuries it was more a counterpoint of rhythm than a counterpoint of part-leading as we know it. Variety of

rhythm was obtained by the lengthening of note (organum);
the truncation of theme (motet); the interchange of voice
(stimmtausch); as well as the breaking up and alternating it
between the different voice parts (hocket), to the shifting even
of the entire rhythm, so that the melody on each re-entry had a
different pattern (isorhythm). Proportional values were also
used to vary the meter of the parts. They did, in fact, about
everything they could do in rhythm and decoration—all due to
individual expression and experiment. It was really a question
of *style* rather than of *form;* though "forms" eventually came
out of them, as in the clausula, motet and hocket.

Proportional devices never made a form, but the voice-leading
enforced by a fresh entry of the text did, urging musicians to
realise that each voice-part had an identity of its own. Yet what
could be more satisfactory to the Renaissance mind in its time,
than the logical imitation of all parts within a single framework,
bringing about the unity of the whole (canon and ricercar)?
Even the effect of the English melodic cantus, when it influenced the Continent, was more that of *style* than of structure.
The verse forms were entirely prosodic. The canzon was an
individualised method of organising a secular part-song; the
toccata, the personal treatment of functional usage; while the
suite was the natural desire to arrange varying dance patterns
within a single mode. Even the eighteenth century sonata was
the outcome of the need to vary a key by modulation, as well as
to balance the main theme by a lighter and more lyrical melody.

How did this affect keyboard music? Firstly, no instrument
had ever been invented for the sole purpose of playing those
rather uninteresting tenors and contratenors. They merely
obliged in those parts, if at all, having styles of their own long
before that. The keyboard instrument was something of an exception. In the modern and perhaps ancient Orient, the function
of an instrument seems to have been mainly: (a) to keep the
pitch or drone, (b) to maintain the notes of a scale pattern,
(c) to decorate or double a theme, (d) to give relief to the
singer between the verses or by alternating with him, and, in

certain types, (e) to mark the accent and rhythm. In the sacred services of the past, relief for the singers was essential, whether by antiphony or by chorus and leader, and it is possible that the ancient organ was used for that purpose, enhanced by the fact it was the loudest and only self-sustaining instrument available.

The organ presented by the Byzantines to the Frankish King, Peppin (AD 757), may have been looked upon not as a new toy, but as an instrument serving a common need—a view supported by the fact that it was used in alternation with the Mass sections and services in the later centuries. Its individual and decorative powers must also have been known. Naturally, the organ style had to be that of a decorative part over a chant portion, curtailed to suit the occasion. Often the "organ book" had so many song transcriptions (Buxheim, nearly two-thirds), that it is reasonable to believe it was also used for secular purposes. Frequently in the organist's handwriting, it was probably looked upon as his property, and could have been carried from one place to another. The didactic monochord and its cousin, the organistrum, was used for teaching singers and keeping the pitch. While its other possible descendant, the clavichord, was later part of a singer's curriculum to train him in the art of music. It was always the private instrument and used by beginners. It cannot be assumed that the cembalo was completely secular, though it became so later.

This alteration should be born in mind when performing the ecclesiastical organ music up to 1530 or later, in that it should be played in conjunction with vocal parts of the Mass, Magnificat or Te Deum, and so on. The solo work that followed later was obviously an extension of this, and could have been played on other keyboard instruments outside the church (as in the ricercar and toccata). Dance music should be grouped into self-made Suites, chosen by selection from a set book, and all in the same or related mode—each pavan being followed by its saltarello and piva, or at a later date by a galliard. The music of the past should be looked upon not as the sole possession of the exotic connoisseur, but as being within the repertories of all great artists. No one would complain of a Scarlatti Sonata in a modern piano recital, though Scarlatti's sonatas were not composed for the modern piano any more than Beethoven's. So why not a Frescobaldi canzon or a Merulo toccata? A few pieces from the old German tablatures would not be out of place. All music needs good playing. The question of adaption, of course, is essential, giving the words "for all kinds of keyboard instruments" a fresh meaning. Assuming the style of ornamentation is understood, there is no reason why a pianist playing sixteenth century music should not insert his own arpeggiation and tremoletti, thus reviving the old tradition of keyboard player as creative improviser. While the noble purist could assist the tradition by bringing forward faithfully reconstructed instruments.

The historical grouping of this book was made as much from "mood" as a sharp division of dates. The style of the late Middle Ages was still that of a polyphonic decoration above or about a theme, as opposed to the imitative counterpoint of the Renaissance. Fifteenth century melody in Germany was still that of the wandering plastic type, in contrast to the square-cut phrasing of the Flemish-Italian Renaissance. The word "Renaissance", however, has a multiplicity of meanings. Some have pushed it back to the Italian *Ars Nova* on account of its secular gaiety and culture, though that spirit was never fully developed in the visual arts until the early fifteenth century. English and Flemish musicians had been working in Italy since the late fourteenth century, but it was not until the second half of the next century that the Renaissance really found its musical expression, which was in essence a combination of Flemish musical weaving with the wealth and splendour of Italy.

At first the Italians were not much in favour with the Flemish counterpoint, preferring their own homophonic frottole and other types as a means of renascent expression. So it was in the coloured madrigal and the harmonic counterpoint of the Mass and motet that the spirit was maintained throughout the sixteenth century. In other countries it developed later. Its learning, again, had two aspects: the reformatory, in North and Middle

Europe, and the artistic, in Italy. Thus, in Germany and England there were residual medieval styles with a reformatory overlay up to about 1500.

Rhythm and scale also played their parts. For a long time the rhythms of the Middle Ages were based on an extension of their metrical patterns, as in the Indo-Arabic traditions. The Renaissance adopted the regularly marked or *divisive* styles, akin to our own and Far Eastern methods. No doubt, the regular phrasing of the popular European part-song played its part. The *Ars Nova* lay in between the two, finally separating Europe from the rest of the world; though it must be remembered that no one felt the need for a bar line until about 1580, when reddish inked lines begin to appear across the printed page. At that date, time values were mostly a subdivision of a basic unit duration, the *tactus,* with the continued beats being molded more by phrase lengths than our own strongly accented bar lines.

In the Renaissance, the harmony and decoration were part of the structure. When the figuration and appoggiatura became part of personal expression, then the style changed into what we have come to know as the Baroque. It is mainly a matter of the feel of the thing, though categorical analysis will no doubt give us a better definition. More satisfactory, perhaps, is the division of music into different countries, where a change in character is readily recognized.

Early musicologists seldom referred to the changing nature of mode throughout History*. Polyphony had pushed the old church modes out of shape by forcing the parts into a different pitch level. Ficta, too, whether by harmonic or melodic necessity, must have created a different modal feeling, which we experience even today in listening to the late Ars Nova or those early German tablatures. Local scales obviously found their way into serious music, and not all scales were octave species, as is demonstrated in many troubadour and minnesinger types. The

* For a discussion of this subject see Ll. S. Lloyd, "History of our Scale," *The Music Review* XIV/3 (August 1953), 173–85.

late Renaissance organised the old church modes forged by
ficta into twelve transposable tones, something like our own
system.The author looks forward to the day when all music
will be examined from a universal point of view. Then, all the
above factors will find their appropriate place.

Lastly, it is a matter of valuation. One cannot say too much
without writing a new book. My examples, like much of that age,
could have been improved upon. It seems that the Robertsbridge
dances might have derived from a harp or psaltery (kanoun)
music. They have that flavour. The *Summa Musicae* (c. 1330)
hints at the existence of tablatures for open and stopped strings.
Many of the items of the Faenza 117 are as difficult to play as
they are to interpret; but considering the extensiveness of the
manuscript, one's approach must be humble. Then, why always
organ? The cembalo was in common use by 1400. The early
German tablatures may also seem strange on first hearing, on
account of their austere nature, though they probably represent
what was normal in Germany at the turn of the fourteenth
century. It would be interesting indeed were a musicologist to
be transported back in time, to have him tell us all he heard and
saw there: his history book would probably be quite different
from our own. Notation never gives us the true rhythm and
colour. Had it not been for the gramophone, the study of
Oriental music would have been largely a closed book. The
trouble today is that we are presented with the good, bad and
indifferent in one heap, and are expected to sort it out. We are
lucky, then, in having the complete Buxheim Book in modern
notation; which, with the equally important *Fundamentum* of
Paumann, represents all that is best in German Gothic keyboard
music of the fifteenth century. The pausae or clausulae were
cadential exercises on a group or formula of notes. The preambula, which were never really based on existing materials, were more individual. The fact that they were always
written on a note of the natural hexachord ($c-a$), yet transposable in other modes, means that they could only be transposed to pitches that need no chromatic alteration save that of

b-flat. The term *redeuntes* means a "returning" of the tenor to
the original keynote, the other parts following the general pattern. In passing, it could be mentioned that the so-called mordent in those manuscripts could often be played as

since Buchner (c. 1513) states that the first note was slightly
held, the auxiliary ones being repeated two or three times;
though the more modern variety of mordent may also have been
known.

It is important to realise that most German tablatures up to
1530 or later were probably made for students or those not
readily able to improvise on a theme; though those books obviously show what was best at that period. The fact that many of
these early performers were blind, as in certain Oriental traditions, may mean that we shall never know the finer points of
their performance.

Rather different were the English manuscripts of that time
(hidden during World War II), which later revealed items of
striking individuality, as in their ornate church music. The singular Attaingnant books could have been given wider treatment
in my text; though I still think that their dance forms were their
highest attainment. Further enthusiasm could have been expressed for the Paulomimes. Of all the names of the mid-six-
teenth century, that of Cabezón stands out as uppermost both
in colour and ingenuity. My love of the Italians still stands
firm. If their general weakness was the adherence to certain
cliches and formulas, their finest achievements showed resplend-
ent qualities that did much to mold the music of the future. It
is a mistake, then, to judge the MS toccatas of Giovanni Gabrieli as representative, when they were most probably employed
as instruction in finger technique. The difficulty at the time of
writing this book was in knowing when to stop. It should have
stopped at 1600. After that there is such a quantity of good
music, that it deserved a study of its own.

If there is any weakness in this book—and I know there are many—it is on the side of underestimation. If I gave the Italians more due than the English, I felt that the latter had been given a fairer treatment by Fellowes, Glyn, and others. Perhaps the greatest omission was the slip of not having included Yvonne Rokseth's formulative work, *La Musique d'orgue au XVᵉ siècle* (1930), in the bibliography. Quite naturally she never mentioned anything of mine in the *New Oxford History of Music*. The statement that the Spaniards may have had some influence on chromatic usage in the sixteenth century could have been true, but the real force was the ancient Greeks. Theory books were full of the supposed enharmonic and chromatic modes. While the Florentine string accompanied monody, though local in the solo madrigal, was in direct imitation of the stringed lyre accompaniment. Some authors have hinted that the variation was common before the Spanish and English items. Variation on a theme as a concrete section was different from a mere variant of something, which existed throughout the ages. The printed variation in Italy and Germany was rare (and that mostly lute), but the professional *divisions* were probably universal.

Gone are the days when people thought this music dull and meaningless. The modern musician has a better chance of becoming acquainted with it than ever before. The church still lacks the enthusiasm to present us with the works of Perotin and his associates, as well as with the Masses of Dufay and later composers in their intended surroundings, where the organ settings could be heard in their right perspective. Either music has value for us or it has not—otherwise all analysis is quite useless. Shakespeare said: "If Music be the food of Love, play on"—and I doubt if he cared, or knew, whether the theme was in canon, canzon or contrary motion. To rephrase Bergson's statement, "the future has yet to gnaw its way into the past."

Kew, Richmond.   G. S. Bedbrook

PREFACE TO THE FIRST EDITION

A full account of keyboard music from the earliest records to the beginning of the baroque period cannot be expected in a volume of this size. Full justice cannot be done even to the major works, so immense is the material at hand. To the average musician and even to many who are highly trained, the music of the Middle Ages and to a large extent that of the Renaissance is unknown territory. Yet the fields of composition therein are so vast and varied that in none is it possible not to find something of interest. This book deals only with keyboard music, and the reader is asked to bear in mind the nature and extent of the rest of the contemporary music. Many no doubt think of keyboard music as going no farther back than the singular productions of Byrd and Bull, yet from the turn of the fourteenth century, at the very least, there was a never interrupted stream of compositions.

Since the second half of the nineteenth century German scholars have written volume after volume on the music of the Middle Ages and Renaissance, followed by an almost equal number of transcriptions into modern notation, in which the keyboard music has been given a reasonable share. The subject was taken up by the musical historians of France, England and Italy, and is now a favourite field for the industrious scholarship of the America of to-day. Few of the major works, however, have been written in English, and most of the music collections, always expensive, are normally unprocurable. While true understanding can come only from first-hand knowledge, the author has endeavoured to pass on his experience by representing what he feels to be the best and most typical of each period.

The assertion may as well be made at this moment that this music of the past, including that of the Middle Ages, is not properly regarded as archaic or experimental, but must be considered as no less perfect in its own way than that of later musicians. This applies not to vocal compositions only, but also to keyboard. Pianists and organists have been slow to appreciate both the backward reach of their tradition in European history and the finesse and quality of the older music. Fifteenth-century organ composition has a charm of its own, once the nature of the style is grasped, while the keyboard music of the Renaissance is a mine of riches only waiting to be discovered. Even music of the baroque period, so varied and so intense in its expression, is not yet fully appreciated. It is for this reason that my book has been written, and with the hope that after this introduction some will seek out and perform the music for themselves. The terms Medieval and Renaissance have been used throughout this work in a musical sense rather than with an exact historic connotation. Music as an art developed somewhat later than other forms of culture.

It is regretted that the examples from which I quote cannot be given in full, but I hope that an anthology of the composers mentioned will follow the present book to enlarge the glimpses here afforded of the glories that lie hidden in the undiscovered centuries of music, the value of which may one day be placed on a level with those of the more commonly recognized periods of the art.

G. S. BEDBROOK

LONDON 1947

ACKNOWLEDGMENTS

I am indebted to the following for permission to reproduce various Plates in this volume: the Directors of the British Museum, Plates I, IV, X, XII and the Frontispiece; the Bodleian Library, Oxford, Plates VI, VII, IX and Ex. LII; the Curtis Institute of Music, Philadelphia, U.S.A., Plate III; the Stiftsbibliothek, St. Gallen, Plate V; and Messrs. W. F. Mansell for Fratelli Alinari of Florence for the reproduction of the Merulo portrait, Plate VIII. For kind permission to quote the numerous examples in this work, I am indebted to Messrs. G. Ricordi & Co., Ex. XLII, LXXVIIa; Novello & Co., Ltd., and the Oxford University Press, for Ex. CIV–CVII, CXVI–CXIX; Schott & Co., Ltd., Ex. I, XXXIII, XLV, LXXV; British Continental Music Agencies, Ltd., Ex. LXXVIIb, and the agents of Breitkopf & Härtel for Ex. XI, XII, LXXI–LXXIV, LXXVIII–LXXXa and XCIX; and to Messrs. John Sherratt & Son for allowing me to quote the passage from C. Hughes' *Shakespeare's Europe* on page 67.

I must also express my gratitude for the information supplied by the Directors and Librarians of the following Institutes and Libraries: the Royal Conservatory of Music, Brussels; Augsburg Municipal Library; the Munich State Library; the National Library, Vienna; the Leipzig State Library; the Hessian State Museum, Darmstadt; the Conservatory of Music, Bologna; the National Museum, Naples; the National Library of St. Mark's, Venice; the Society for the Musical History of the Netherlands, The Hague, Holland; the Breslau Library (Wroclaw); the Institute of Spain, London; the University of Basle: particularly to Dr. Isräel of the Landesbibliothek, Kassel (Marburg); Dr. Peter Wackernagel of the Berlin State Library; Mr. Leonard Ellinwood of the Library of Congress, Washington; and Dr. Willi Apel of Boston, Mass. Special thanks are due to Mon. Giuseppe De Biasio (Parroco) for kindly sending me information and a photograph of Giovanni Gabrieli's tomb at San Stefano's, Venice, as well as to Dr. Van den Sigtenhorst Meyer for allowing me to see photostats of some Sweelinck originals. The same will apply to the University of Basle for photographing some works of Andrea and Giovanni Gabrieli, and to the Directors of the Archives of State, Venice, for photographing a document relating to the organists of St. Mark's. I am greatly indebted to my friends Mr. C. H. Trevor and Mr. Robert Donington for reading over my proofs and musical examples, to Mr. Richard Capell for suggesting some useful revision in preparing this work, and to Mr. Raymond Ellis for assisting me with the Index. Many kind thanks are also offered to my friend Mr. A. P. H. Saul, and to the Rev. G. J. Cuming and Mr. Francis Clough for giving me useful information about the gramophone records of this period, as well as to Prof. Gerald Abraham for allowing me to make use of the B.B.C. Gramophone Library. Above all I wish to express my sincerest appreciation to all those who have given encouragement and sympathy with this work, with the earnest hope that the material inscribed will afford some guidance and assistance to all lovers of music, as well as those who have already accepted the traditions of the past.

G. S. B.

CONTENTS

PART I—THE MEDIEVAL PERIOD

CHAPTER I: THE ANCIENT AND MEDIEVAL ORGAN

CHAPTER II: THE FOURTEENTH CENTURY

CHAPTER III: THE FIFTEENTH CENTURY

PART III—THE NORTH EUROPEAN SCHOOLS AND THE BEGINNINGS OF THE BAROQUE

LIST OF ILLUSTRATIONS

LIST OF ILLUSTRATIONS

PART I

THE MEDIEVAL PERIOD

THE ANCIENT AND MEDIEVAL ORGAN

ORIGINS OF THE TERM ORGAN. THE USE OF THE ORGAN IN THE MIDDLE AGES

It is erroneous to imagine that all the early music of Europe was vocal, and that instrumental music is a late development. Musical instruments have been used from time immemorial by every race and people, and although the keyboard is of comparatively recent date its predecessors, the levered organ and keyed monochord, have a very ancient origin. The organ itself, from which the keyboard apparently developed, probably came from Asia via Rome or was, as some authorities state, introduced into Europe by the Arabs.[1] The Roman hydraulus or water organ appears to have been held in great esteem. Claudian (c. 400) speaks of it as a full-sounding instrument, capable of rapid execution, 'with nimble fingers making deep murmurs.'[2] The Byzantines, too, gave the organ special favour.

Within the Christian era there are numerous early references to organs, some of which seem to have had considerable power. St. Jerome speaks of an organ at Jerusalem which with '12 brazen pipes' and '15 smith's bellows', could be heard on the Mount of Olives. To the audience of the time the effect was probably not forbidding, for a later instrument at Rome is spoken of as emitting 'brilliant and pleasing tones'. The earliest reliable accounts, however, start about the seventh century. The keys in those days consisted mostly of buttons, sliders or metal strips, and often more than one organist was employed at the keyboard.

The largest organ of the early Middle Ages of which we have record was that at Winchester (c. 850), which was evidently both powerful and extensive. It had 400 pipes, with 70 men at the

[1] See Farmer (H. G.), 'The Organ of the Ancients from Eastern Sources.' (*Studies in Oriental Musical Instruments*, 1) 1931.

[2] See Galpin (Canon Francis), *Reliquary*, July, 1904, and *Scientific American* 19th Nov., 1904.

bellows at full blast. It is described as 'reverberating and echoing in every direction', so that 'no one was able to draw near and hear the sound, but that he had to stop with his hands his gaping ears'. The upper range, however, was probably far softer.

Some of the larger organs down to about 1300 apparently had rather awkward levers, ranging from 3″ to 6″ long, to control the notes. These probably decreased in size and awkwardness as time went on. Their drop was deep, and they were hit by the clenched fist. This technique may strike us as difficult; but there is no reason to suppose it more so to the musician brought up to such instruments, than playing the pedals of our organs or—in a closer analogy—the heavy keyboard of a modern carillon. Organs, however, were not all of this nature. Many of the instruments depicted in manuscripts had lighter keys of sliders or metal strips. Later, springs or weights were used, which must have greatly assisted the playing of even the largest organs. With the development of the keyboard in the thirteenth century, the smaller instruments became very popular.

The close relationship between the words organ and organum —the latter one of the earliest-known terms for a composition in more than one part—suggests the derivation of that compositional style from an instrumental performance. The subject, however, is complicated. Let us first note the historical evidence. Organum, as a composition, appears to have been first described as a chant accompanied or followed in parallel movement at a 5th or 4th below and doubled at the octave, as well as by certain oblique motions arising from and proceeding to a unison. ('Musica Enchiriadis', c. 850.)[1] Even when all the voices of this composition proceeded in contrary motion, the basic principle was still that of 1st, 5th or 4th and 8ve. It seems that at one time the upper voice-parts were divided into notes of shorter values, the lowest voice assuming those of the longest values. This type of composition, in which extremely prolonged tenor notes in 'measureless' rhythm supported an upper voice in shorter and 'measured' rhythm, was

[1] There are earlier accounts, but the descriptions are vague. See Gustave Reese's *Music in the Middle Ages*, p. 252 (1941).

called 'organum purum', and although it developed into forms with 3 or 4 voices, in which some parts were 'measured' and other parts 'unmeasured', some sections in note-against-note style, others with the upper parts in lesser values, it still retained the term 'organum'.

The Greek word 'organon' originally meant a tool, and hence a musical instrument, usually one of many strings. It is well known that the organistrum or hurdy-gurdy sounded a 1st, 5th and 8ve for every note that was played, and its name refers no doubt to the early medieval consonance. It also appears that the broad-bodied types of fiddles (rubebes or broad vièles) caused the bow to touch the other strings at a 5th or 8ve, or as a sort of drone. This probably occurred with the bowed lyras (rottas), crwths and other varieties. Medieval Arabs sounded a simultaneous 4th on their lutes by way of ornamentation. The mere fact of passing the hands across the strings in the playing of such instruments as harps, lyres and psalteries obviously made for a kind of harmony. Harmony of the 5th or 4th and 8ve has been known in both the ancient and modern Orient, as well as among primitive races.

More important than the question of harmony is the aspect of heterophony. It is obvious that when more than one voice or instrument plays the same melody, one part, particularly with a voice and instrument, will tend to deviate from the other. This not only happens with the most primitive races, but also in cultured Eastern countries, the instrumental part by its very nature becoming decorative or ornamental. The idea of a florid 'part' above the original melody—most early instruments were probably played above the voice—may have tempted musicians to call a similar 'part' or composition 'organal', and hence 'organum'. The earliest accounts speak of the organal voice as accompanying the original melody (vox principalis) and that 'organum' was merely a method of 'decorating' the chant. In the 'Musica Enchiriadis' and 'Micrologus' (c. 1000), the organal part was below the 'principalis', except where it was doubled at the octave, when it occurred as the highest voice. After the Winchester Troper manuscript, however, it always became the upper voice (c. 1050). The comparative scarcity of accounts and music in this period makes exact knowledge difficult. The earliest written organa are generally in a note-against-note style most suited to ecclesiastical sanction, and may have been the final acceptance of an ancient practice of secular music; and the above theses, the first scientific explanation of it. In fact, many authorities think that the florid organum may have antedated or certainly co-existed with the parallel type. The florid upper voice was definitely predominant from about 1100. The singing in parallel 4th or 5ths, or even 3rds or fauxbourdon, was probably very ancient, being within the natural range of mixed voices, yet the decorative instrumental blending must have existed from very remote times.

It is possible, then, that the organ proper originally accompanied the chant at a 4th or 5th above or below the voices, or that it sounded a 5th and 8ve with each of its notes in a sort of 'mixture', like the 'organistrum'.[1] But considering that the organ always appears to have been used alternately with the singers in later times, it is conceivable that the organ retained its name from the type of composition played on it, i.e. a florid upper voice over an elongated tenor. It is remarkable that the earliest known forms of organ compositions, i.e. the Preambula, Pausae and Clausulae, with their long-drawn-out tenor notes and descant upper voices, should have such a similarity to the vocal organa of earlier medieval times. The fact that the early organ frequently had a deep drone-note, to judge by contemporary illustrations, may have encouraged this type of composition. Compare Ex. I with Ex. II:

Ex. I (Benedicamus Domino)

---

[1] To judge by the measurement of certain ranks of pipes of the Hydraulus organ (dated A.D. 228) discovered at the site of a Roman encampment near Budapest in 1931, it seems that they sounded together a unison, 5th and 8ve. (See Canon Galpin's *A Textbook of European Musical Instruments*, p. 177 (1937).)

Ex. IIa (Preambulum on g) (Buxheim Book)
Ex. IIb (Preambulum on C) (Ileborgh)

A certain Conradus, a Cistercian of the fourteenth century (1340), states that the word 'organum' referred not only to the organ but was a generic term for any instrument, adding that a composition (cantelenam), when played on an organ itself may also be called 'organum'. (See *Musical Quarterly*, New York, July and Oct. 1942.) In 1397 Bartholomaeus de Glanville writes: 'Organum is a general name of all instrumentes of musyk, and is nethelesse specyally a propryte to the instrument that is made of many pipes, and blowe(n) with belows.' (Sir John Hawkins' account of 'De proprietatibus rerum', p. 269.)

The term 'organista'—as when the famous Notre Dame composer Leonin was called 'optimus organista'—meant a composer of organa. The word for the organist proper was either 'pulsator organorum' (beater or striker of the organ notes) or, later, 'organator'; just as the term 'estrumentor' was later used for the instrumental player as distinguished from the singer. Thus in Paris we hear of Maître Boudoin l'Orgueneur and Jehan l'Orgueneur (c. 1300). Of the latter we still possess two songs.

MEDIEVAL COMPOSITIONS. THE ROBERTSBRIDGE FRAGMENT

It is not exactly known for what purpose medieval organs were used. It appears that at church services they were played between the singing, as it is known that they were used to do in later centuries. Aelred's (twelfth century) famous complaint asking why there were 'so many organs and cymbala (chime-bells?)' in the divine service is evidence enough that they were in common use.[1] Aegidius (*c.* 1250) states that they were used for 'proses, sequences and hymns'. With the easier and later keyboards, however, and with the smaller class of organ, they may have acted as a tenor to the motets of the time.

Failing a real knowledge of the organ and instrumental playing of that period, we can give but a brief and rough summary of the composition of that day.

The earliest types of polyphonic composition, i.e. the organum and the conductus (a composition with a rhythmic text in the tenor and two voices more or less conforming to its rhythm above it), were written in score-form as to-day. The words were written under the tenor only, the upper voices using possibly the same text or syllable. On the other hand the motet had, as a rule, all its voices separate, the tenor generally being placed at the bottom of the manuscript, the other and upper parts being on opposite sides of the page at the top. This was the usual way of writing secular songs through the thirteenth, fourteenth and fifteenth centuries. In the Motet, of course, each upper part had a text of its own.

The motet, the last type of composition of the so-called Notre Dame, Chartres and other Schools of Music, consisted of the addition of two voices (motetus and triplum) to a tenor, which was made by cutting a chosen ecclesiastical chant, or occasionally a secular song, into a certain rhythmic pattern. As it was textless, save for the title of the chant or song from which it was taken, it has often been conceived that it was instrumental, particularly since there is evidence that the later or more secular motets were accompanied by an instrument of some sort (probably vièle or other stringed instrument). It is more likely that the title of the tenor may have served as a guide to the chant to be performed; which in all probability was known and sung from memory, even if cut into a certain pattern. There is also evidence that these tenors

[1] Unde quaeso cessantibus jam typis et figuris, unde in Ecclesia tot organa, tot cymbala? Ad quid, rogo, terribilis ille follium flatus, tonetrui potius fragorum, quam vocis exprimens suavitatem?—stans intrae vulgus sonitum follium, crepitum cymbalorum, harmoniam fistularum, tremens attonitusque miratur. (Aelred, *Speculum Charitatis*, Lib. II, 23.)

were sung to the first syllable, i.e. Om . . . nes (Omnes), so that a textless passage in a piece of medieval music does not necessarily imply the employment of any instrument whatever. Besides, the writing of those large and often illuminated musical manuscripts was a laborious and costly business. They were designed to be read only by about six to nine singers, and this would mean that another book would have had to be prepared for a separate instrumentalist like the organist. There are hundreds of manuscripts of the compositions of the time in the forms of organum, conductus and motet, but no copy or mention of an organist's book is known to us until the late fourteenth century, and then only for 'alternative' playing.

With secular composition, however, we are on much better ground. It seems that a dance-form known as the Estampie and its varieties were played on the vièle and other instruments. Such pieces have been found in both one and two parts.[1] But there are also three specimens in a manuscript known as the Robertsbridge Fragment (ADD 28550, Brit. Mus.) which, on account of having a few letters for the tenor instead of ordinary notes, are thought to be in organ tablature.[2]

Ex. III (Estampie No. 2)

The estampies found in this famous fragment are often supposed to be for the large organ, but they may, on the strength of their apparently secular character, have also been played on the smaller or portative organ, or even on the 'eschaquier' (the earliest form

---

[1] Sir John Stainer, *Early Bodleian Music,* Vol. I, Facs; Vol. II, Transcriptions, 1901. Wooldridge, *Early English Harmony,* Vol. I, Facs., 1897; Vol. II, Transcriptions, 1913. Pierre Aubry, *Estampies et Danses Royales,* 1906.

[2] A Tablature is a system of writing for instruments such as organ and lute. The organ, consisting of a single stave with letters underneath for the tenor notes, seems to have been mostly used in Germany during the fifteenth and sixteenth centuries.

of clavichord). (See Chapter II, p.13). They are often considered
to date from about 1350. The remaining three compositions are
based on some works in the Roman de Fauvel (c.1316–20). The
general crudeness of the style, compared with the mid fourteenth-
century continental practice, however, seems rather to point to
about 1325. The handwriting is definitely English, and on the early
side of the fourteenth century, but the music is only bound up
with the manuscripts belonging to the Robertsbridge Abbey.

The great interest of this manuscript lies in its containing the
first known work for a keyboard. There are six pieces. The three

Ex. IV

(Adesto Sancta)

estampies are probably instrumental solos; the others are obviously
early keyboard arrangements of motets, with rather standardized
and possibly commonplace figurations. They are taken from the
'Tribum-Quoniam secta' and 'Firmissime-Adesto Sancta Trinitas'
motets (possibly De Vitri's) of the Roman de Fauvel manuscript,
and probably represent the music performed in alternation with
the singing in the Mass of that time.[1] As music, though not of great
artistic value to judge by modern transcriptions, they have a gay
lilting character which gives them a quaint medieval, if not
English, charm. The harmony is often elementary, though there
is occasional movement in 6ths, and the structure, strange to our
ears, is of the wandering, plastic medieval phraseology. Though of

[1] The fact that they also possess the words of the text may mean that these
pieces were used for accompanying the voices. This, however, is a unique case.

ecclesiastical origin, they appear to be secular in character, and probably belong to a secularized version of the ecclesiastical compositions that became popular with the keyboard music of the Renaissance, particularly since they are included among the dances named.

That these dance-forms were played on an organ seems confirmed by accounts we have of that famous lover of instrumental music, King John I of Aragon (1387–96). (See p. 14.) Desirous of obtaining the services of a certain famous organist and 'his portatives', he is stated to have been particularly anxious to get hold of 'his book in which were written the estampies and other pieces he played'.

CHAPTER II

THE FOURTEENTH CENTURY

The Organ in the Ars Nova Period

By about 1300 the keyboard of the larger organs had taken on a more manageable shape. The keys were now much smaller, though often as much as one and a half inches apart. There were as many as twenty or thirty keys all told, and chromatic keys had come in. Pedals, too, were used by about 1300. The white notes are said to have been played by the wrist, the black by the 1st, 2nd and 3rd fingers together. A crude but still an improved technique! This probably refers, of course, to the church organ or 'organum magnum'. The ninfale or 'portative' organ, a smaller and much more manageable instrument, was the one mainly used. It could be carried and held by the arm or on the knee. The rather larger instrument, the 'positive',[1] was placed on a table or ledge. In most instances, the bellows of the portative were blown by the left hand, while the right hand played the keys, much as a modern piano-accordion is played. In the case of the positive organ, a servant or friend blew the bellows for the executant. In this and the following century, the small 'portative' organ was what the pianoforte is to-day, a domestic instrument given more to lyrical than to sacred music.

We hear of many kings and courts possessing a number of organs. Charles V of France had three, Philip the Bold several. The small ones, which were the most numerous, were naturally high pitched by reason of the shortness of the pipes, and they must have produced a quiet, fluty sort of tone, more suited to lyrical compositions than to the music we commonly associate with the organ. Some organs, however, reached a great size, such as the famous one at Halberstadt, erected in 1361. It had three manuals

[1] The portative was easily movable. The positive organ was movable, but generally stationary in one part of the church.

and a pedal-board, and ten men were required to work the bellows. As the keys were about one and a half inches apart, the movement from note to note must have been difficult by modern standards. Many ranks of pipes were fixed to the first descant manual and pedals, as in most of the earlier organs where all ranks of pipes spoke at once, but in the second descant and bass manual only the diapason stops acted; thus providing for a contrast, though, indeed, a violent one. It is said that two-part playing was possible on these manuals, perhaps with an occasional pedal note. Specified, it may be said to have run as follows:

1st DESCANT MANUAL.	2nd DESCANT MANUAL.
Hintersatz (Mixture) 32 to 56 ranks. *Praestant (Open Diapason).*	*Principal (Open Diapason).*
BASS MANUAL.	PEDALS.
Principal.	*Principal Hintersatz (16 to 24 ranks).*

According to Van der Mueren, there was an organ at Antwerp in 1394, which possessed:

Open Fluit (4 ft.)	Quintadeen
Dulcian	Sesquialter
Octaf	Mixture
Rorefluit	Regalis

See Mueren (Van der) 'Het Orgel in der Nederlanden' (Leuven), 1931.

THE CLAVICHORDIUM AND CLAVICYMBALUM

The medieval clavichordium and clavicymbalum, the forerunners of the later clavichord and harpsichord, can be traced back to the thirteenth century. They must have had a still earlier origin. Monochords, which eventually increased from the one string to several, seem to have had keys attached to them. Jean de Muris (1323) mentions a so-called monochord instrument with nineteen strings. It is curious that the psaltery, a rhomboidal instrument with wire strings, was at one time called a 'cimbalo' or 'cymbal' in England. An instrument called the Echiquier or Eschaquier, called in one poem 'Eschaquier d'Engleterre', and possibly of English invention, was presented by Edward III to John II of France (1350–64) while a prisoner of his. King John I of Aragon (1387–96) also has a special interest for us, for he seems to have been the first eminent patron of keyboard music, showing an exceptional liking for the echiquier and small organ. He possessed many kinds of instruments, and is said to have taken into his service anybody who could play them with skill, as well as sending enquiries to foreign kings and courts for the purchase or exchange of instruments and players. He described the echiquier as an instrument 'like an organ that sounds the strings'. A very clavichord indeed! The word 'eschaquier' may have come from the Arabic word 'al-shaqira', a box-shaped stringed instrument, and it may have reached England through the rise of Arabic studies which took place here. But many suppose it to derive from an old word meaning 'to check' (i.e. the jacks), or simply the 'jacks' themselves.

The names 'clavicordium' and 'clavicymbolum' do not occur until the next century (i.e. 1404), when they are mentioned in a list of instruments by the Minnesinger, Eberhardus Cersne von Minden. They must have been thinner in tone than the organ and less sustaining, and this no doubt accounts for the organ's greater popularity. See P. James' *Early Keyboard Instruments*, 1930.

THE FLORENTINES. FRANCESCO LANDINI. SOME ACCOUNT OF ORGAN PLAYING IN FRANCE

Some of the earliest records of regular organists come from Italy. We hear of Zucchetti's playing and his becoming chief organist of St. Mark's, Venice, in 1318, to be followed by Francesco Pesaro in 1337 and Giovanni Dattalo in 1368. The greatest reputation of them all, particularly for performance on the 'organetto' or portative organ, was that of the Florentine musician Francesco Landini (1325–97). Born blind and of noble parentage, he possessed a wide culture and was a poet and philosopher, as well as one of the finest composers of his time. Besides the organ, he played the lute, guitar, flute, and an instrument of his own construction called the 'serena serenorum'. Most of his fame, however, seems to have rested on his organetto playing, and his greatly admired vocal, and instrumentally accompanied, part-songs.

Despite his infirmity he enjoyed the most cultivated company, together with a great popularity, in the delightful atmosphere of art-loving fourteenth-century Florence. At the Venice festival of 1364 he entered into competition with Pesaro, the organist of St. Mark's, in the presence of many notables, including the poet Petrarch. Although he lost in the actual contest with Pesaro, which was perhaps on a larger or positive organ, the nature of which Pesaro was probably the more familiar with, he being the established church organist there, Landini was crowned with laurels for the excellence of his poetry (songs?) by King Pietro of Cyprus.

All Landini's compositions are written in two or three parts, after the manner of the verse structures of the time, such as the Madrigal[1] and Ballata, as well as the early canonic part-song known

Ex. V (Orsun gentili spiriti)

as the Caccia.[2] All are of a lyrical nature, the poetry of Dante and Petrarch often being set to music during this period. The Ballata, like other forms, such as the Estampita and Rondeau, appears to have been both sung and danced. (See the conclusion

[1] Originally a pastoral poem set to music.
[2] Literally hunting-pieces; but they are usually lively compositions about topical events mingled with a poetical background. The upper voices were generally in canon above the normal tenor.

of the day's diversions in Boccaccio's *Decameron*.) Practically all Landini's ballatas have an uppermost solo voice-part, while the lower voices (tenor and contratenor) remain with no text, as in a large number of the secular songs of the fourteenth and fifteenth centuries. (See Ex. V.)

Purely instrumental dance-forms, such as the solo Estampita and Saltarello, are to be found among the works of Florentine composers. (ADD 29987, Brit. Mus.), e.g.

Ex. VI

(La Manfredina) (1st Section)

It is likely, then, that it was either these or some arrangement of his songs, or both, that Landini performed on his organetto; so we may judge by a description of his playing: 'The whole assembly is excited by his organ playing, the young dance and sing, and the old hum. He draws wonders from the little organ, even the birds cease their song and draw near to listen.'

A poem written to celebrate the skill of a certain musician (Il Sollazzo), states that 'the organ instead of accompanying the voices . . . alternates with them'. We are also told that this same musician played a certain motet from the Ivrea MS. (El Molin de Paris) on a Flemish organ,[1] as well as some pieces by Giovanni da Cascia and Jacopo da Bologna (two important Florentine musicians) on the harp.[2] This probably signifies an arrangement of some sort, possibly not unlike those of the early English and German tablatures. It is quite possible that vocal ballatas and the like were either accompanied by an instrumental tenor, or re-

---

[1] Gustave Reese, *Music in the Middle Ages*, p. 384, 1941.

[2] Notation in score-form, as in certain ecclesiastical music, could be read with difficulty perhaps (see frontis. of Farmer's *Music of Medieval Scotland* for solo voice part), but the average part-songs could not. Many of the works of the sixteenth-century Italian organists, however, appear to have been printed in score.

PLATE I

MINIATURE OF KING DAVID
AT POSITIVE ORGAN
French Psalter c.1300

14TH CENTURY POSITIVE ORGAN
From an Italian Choral Book

arranged so as to form organ and other instrumental solos. In some cases instruments would take the place of voices. There is even evidence, too, that the tenor was used as a sort of continuo (the word 'tenor' denoting the holding part, i.e. *teneo*—I hold), as at a later time.

A frequently presumed organ arrangement of Landini's 'Questa Fanciulla'[1] is thought to belong to the fifteenth century, but it may preserve for us something of the sort of thing played. It is written with a textless tenor and cantus part, as was fairly common with the music of the time.

About 150 of Landini's compositions are known. The bulk of them were not transcribed until quite recently.[2] Like the rest of his Florentine contemporaries and to an even greater degree, Landini is smoother and sweeter than his predecessors. His melodies are well-phrased by the standard of his time, and his sense of cadence and smoothness of harmony is distinctly conveyed. His compositions when properly reviewed reveal a freshness and sweetness of character in keeping with the atmosphere of early Renaissance Italy, the music of which is unknown to the general musician. His skill as a player on the organetto (ninfale) was widely recognised, and both his portrait and tombstone show him with a small ninfale in his left arm.

Guillaume de Machaut (*c.* 1300–1377), the greatest French composer of this period, speaks of the organ as 'the king of instruments'. He says that his ballades (another verse form) can be played on an organ, 'cornemusa' (bagpipes?), and other instruments, as well as being sung. As in earlier centuries, so now there are so many textless tenor parts in both the sacred and secular motets of this period that it is often assumed they were played by instruments, including no doubt the portative organ. The tenors of these medieval compositions may, however, as I have previously suggested, have been vocalized, though the general smoothness of the longer notes in the lower parts may perhaps have induced musicians to play them instrumentally.

[1] *Fonds Nouv*: acq. 6771 (Bibl. Nat.).
[2] Leonard Ellinwood, *The Works of Francesco Landini*, 1939.

B.K.M.

It is said that the small organ (portative) was frequently used to fill in parts, to hold players together, or to relieve them by interludes, as well as to enrich and embellish certain sections. (See Lang's *Music in Western Civilization*, 1942.) The positive may also have done the same thing. As for the larger church organs, special books were written for the organist to play in alternation with the different sections of the sung Mass or Service. In an account of Notre Dame in the early fifteenth century, it is stated that the organist's book 'Liber Organistoris' was re-written on account of 'its ancientness' (i.e. its archaic style of notation) by May 18th, 1416. This indicates that it must have been used throughout the fourteenth century, and perhaps earlier. When Henry de Saxe became organist of Notre Dame in the early part of the fourteenth century, he was expected to play for early Vespers, 23 Feast Days, also during the Kyrie, Gloria, Sequence, Sanctus and Agnus Dei. (See *Musical Quarterly*, Oct. 1925.) A fourteenth-century manuscript connected with the Sagan Monastery states that the 'clerics' sang the Gradual, three brothers the Alleluia verses—'unless played by the organs'—a hint at the alternative playing of later periods. It is known that a 'Mary-Mass' was performed on an organ in 1384, as well as a 'Beata-Virgine-Gaudeamus' in 1414. Bartholomaeus de Glanville (1397), again, says that the organ was used for the 'proses, sequences, and ympnes' (hymns) in the divine service. (See p. 8).

CHAPTER III

THE FIFTEENTH CENTURY

FIFTEENTH-CENTURY ORGANS AND ORGANISTS

During the fifteenth century there was a general improvement in the mechanism of the organ—keys, pedals, stops and wind supply. The keyboard in the fifteenth century became far more manageable. The keys were generally about an inch to one and a half inches wide. The black keys lay behind the white, and the keyboard thus assumed a more reasonable size, akin to what we know. Keys were played by the thumb and first two fingers together, and a fifth could easily be stretched on even the widest arrangement of notes. Stops at first were mostly fixed or compound. The first known solo stop was a 'flute' of about 1400. One organ in 1429 had 2500 pipes. The largest pipe of a 1441 organ measured 10 in. in diameter and was 28 ft. long. A few years later there was a pipe in France through which a man is said to have been able to crawl. The large organs frequently played independently, and possibly in many parts of the Mass solo, with the positive or stationary organ doing the accompanying. The portatives were still mostly secular.

ITALY (SQUARCIALUPO)

Of the famous Florentine organist Squarcialupo (*fl.* 1430–1480), we know little. He played at the court of Lorenzo de Medici, and was succeeded by Heinrich Isaac in 1485. There is a letter from Squarcialupo to Dufay in existence saying how much he and Lorenzo admired his music—an indication of the close connections between the Italian and early Flemish Schools. Squarcialupo may have had an even greater fame than Landini.[1] The work of Jacobus Viletti (if Italian) in the Buxheim Organ Book[2]

---

[1] See Eitner (R), *Monatshefte fur Musikgeschichte*, Article by O. Kade, 1885.

[2] Eitner says that he was a singer in the Royal Chapel at Naples in 1480. (See Quellen-Lexicon.)

may represent something like his style of organ composition, the two being more or less contemporary. (See p. 31.)

FLANDERS

It is surprising that few examples have been found of organ music and playing throughout the great Flemish periods[1], and we do not know whether Okeghem and Josquin des Prés were themselves organists. It is quite possible that they were familiar with the Italian and German organists of the day. In the illuminated headpiece of the famous Martin-le-France's poem, showing Dufay and Binchois together, there is a fair-sized positive organ by the side of Dufay, and a harp by Binchois; which shows at least that this instrument must have been considered as an appropriate background to perhaps the greatest musician of the time.

GERMANY

Early German Tablatures

Of German keyboard music, on the other hand, we have quite an extensive knowledge from the first quarter of the fifteenth century to the last third. Some early pieces known as the Sagan MS., found in the bindings of some sermons dated 1432, are believed to have been used as arrangements for the Mass round about 1425. There are also a few compositions attached to a series of sermons by Ludolf Wilkin von Winsem dated 1432 (Berlin State Library), as well as one or two pieces found in some interesting tracts in the State Libraries of Munich—'Scripta mathematica et musica' (c. 1436–74 (Cod. Lat. 3963) and Hamburg (dated 1437) (MS. VI, M3225). The Erlanger University Library, again, possesses some important accounts—'Tract de facundo clavicordia', 'Tract de opere organico faciendo et organorum structura' (MS. 729). One of the first comprehensive collections of organ music is that compiled by Brother Adam Ileborgh in 1448, now at the Curtis Institute, N.Y. Some mid-fifteenth-century Mass

[1] See Mueren (Van der) *Het Orgel in der Nederlanden*, 1931; Schering (A), *Die Niedlandische Orgelmesse*, 1912. (See also p. 154 of present book and Dufourcq (N), *Esquisse d'une histoire de l'orgue en France*, 1935.)

'arrangements' in two manuscripts have been found, which belonged to the Dominican Friary at Breslau (*c.* 1430–40 and 1450–60), but perhaps the largest and finest collections of the period are in that famous work, formerly considered unique, the 'Fundamentum Organisandi' of Conrad Paumann (1452), and that amazing volume of pieces known as the Buxheim Organ Book (*c.* 1460). A large number of compositions from these manuscripts[1] have now been brought back to light.

The Sagan, Winsem, and Breslau MSS.

The Sagan manuscript[2] is an early work, and gives us an idea of what went on in the musically backward Germany of the late fourteenth century. Its contents are the presumably conventional organ settings of portions of the Mass ('Et in terra', 'Benedicamus te', 'Glorificamus te'), which, according to definite evidence, were played in alternation with sections sung by the choir. Thus a manuscript[3] connected with the Sagan Monastery states that the usual order was Gradual (organ), Jubilatus (choir), Alleluia (organ) and Alleluia (choir), Pascha Nostrum (1st verse organ), and Alleluia (choir); which agrees with the surviving examples of the period. This Sagan Tablature is an interesting work, for it is a link with the earlier Robertsbridge Fragment (*c.* 1325). It is somewhat grim according to modern standards, and its pieces sound rather primitive to those unaccustomed to medieval melodic progressions. As in most medieval music, the tenor contains the melody, which supports a freely flowing descant in the upper voice, and here again, as in all the earlier types of organ composition, the tenor part is written in rigidly uniform notes of equal value. 'Et in terra' is even more primitive than its companions, though it is not without a certain ascetic charm.

---

[1] (See Leo Schrade, *Die Landschriftliche Überlieferung der ältesten Instrumentalmusik* (1931), and *Die Messe in der Orgel des 15 Jahr. Archiv für Musikforschung* (1936). Fritz Feldmann, *Musik und Musikpflege im mittelälterlichen Schlesien* (1938). 'Ein Tabulatur-fragment des Breslauer Dominikaner-Klosters'—*Zeitschrift für Musikwissenschaft*, XV (1933). Summary in *Musical Quarterly*, July and Oct., 1942.

[2] Breslau I. *Qu.* 438.   [3] Breslau I. *Oct. MS.* 61.

Ex. VII (Et in terra)

'Benedicamus te' has a queer melodic turn of phrase which, although transcribed in semiquavers, was probably played 'lento' in free rhythmic style.

Ex. VIII (Benedicamus te)

These examples give one an idea of the cold, ascetic atmosphere of a remote monastery in medieval Germany, and a certain patience is needed if one would appreciate the meaning of this distant music. Somewhat more regularly patterned is the 'Summum Sanctus' of the Winsem MS. (*c.* 1430)[1], which flows with greater smoothness of phrase:

Ex. IX (Summum Sanctus)

---

[1] Berlin State Library MS. *Theol. Lat. Qu.* 290.

Besides a 'Patrem', a 'Credo' and others, there are also some works with secular canti-firmi, such as the German song 'Wol up ghesellen'. The presence of secular themes does not mean that the music was used for secular purposes. They simply formed the basis of the composition. Sacred works were as often employed for secular use as secular material was for sacred purposes; no hard and fast distinction was thought necessary, as in later times.

Slightly more developed are the compositions of the first Breslau MS. (Qu. 42) (c. 1430–40) which contains some interesting arrangements of certain portions of a plainsong, which were formed into definite sections of the old organum known as 'clausulae'. These simple 'clausulae' on the different degrees of the gamut are in three parts, with a tenor and contratenor as an organal bass instead of a single tenor. They range from *d* to *bb*, including *b♮*.

Ex. X

Clausula (descendens)

The clausulae on single notes were apparently called 'Pausae', as one clausula on *d* is called a 'pausa generalis super D'. These forms, with greatly extended pedal notes, are also called 'Pausae' in Conrad Paumann's 'Fundamentum Organisandi', and presumably come from the same source.

The other Breslau MS. (Qu. 687) (1450–60) brings us up to the Ileborgh Tablature, with hints of the Paumann period, and may be said to represent the end of the early period of German organ music. The tenors of these works are not always so rigidly fixed in notes of equal value, but are given a slight variety of pattern, as in later periods. The melodic line, again, is smoother, and better phrased according to modern standards.

Ex. XI Bon(*us tenor*) leohar(*di*) (Carnificis?)

particularly:

Ex. XII (tenor bonus iij petri)

Beside these settings on sacred themes, there are a number of compositions with song melodies, such as 'Mit ganczem Willin', and 'Der Wynter der wil'; the former of which is to be found again in the Fundamentum of Paumann, as well as in the Buxheim Organ Book and later German manuscripts.

THE ILEBORGH TABLATURE (1448)

Ileborgh's manuscript is an interesting work from an aesthetic as well as an historical point of view. The tablature in question contains 5 short *Preambula* (preambles) and 3 longer *Mensurae*, which were apparently collected by Adam Ileborgh in the year of his rectorate at Standall (1448). He describes them as being 'in the modern manner', which probably refers to the use of a duple notation, or the new method of writing in three parts with greater rhythmic distinction in the upper descant, rather than to the compositions themselves. These are still elementary and on first acquaintance seem somewhat arid, but repeated playing generally

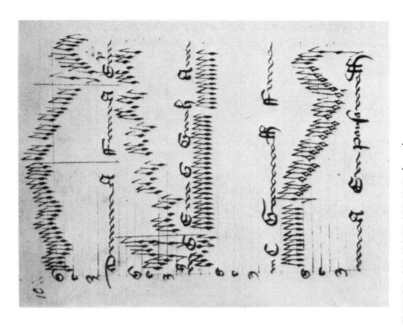

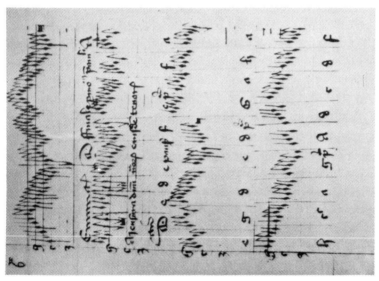

PLATE II

TWO PAGES FROM THE ILEBORGH TABLATURE (1448)

reveals in them a characteristic sweetness. The preambles, at least, must be looked upon as representing one of the earliest known attempts at absolute keyboard music, since they do not seem to draw upon any liturgical material but to have been used simply as a prelude or interlude.

Ex. XIII (Preambulum bonum super C)

Two preambles (Nos. 3 and 5) are for the manuals, No. 4 for pedals or manuals ('pedale sive manuale'). It is interesting to note, that only preambles Nos. 1 and 4 have the usual letters for the tenor notes, the rest having only longs and breves, which indicates that the letters of this tablature, at least, referred to the pedals. It may not have been strictly so with the later ones. These Mensurae have some extraordinarily interesting figuration

Ex. XIV

which tempts one to feel that they may have been adapted from clavichord pieces (e.g. a possible 'bebung').

The Mensurae are compositions based on a 'song' tenor in measured rhythms, such as 'Frowe al myn hoffen an dyr lyed' ('My lady, all my hope depends on you').

Ex. XV

CONRAD PAUMANN

THE FUNDAMENTUM ORGANISANDI

Among the number of names of organists appearing in the fifteenth century, the most famous is that of Conrad Paumann (1410–1473), described by the poet Hans Rosenpluet as 'the master of masters'. He was also a skilled player on the lute, flute, rebec, citole and krum-horne (cromorne),[1] though it is particularly as an organist and composer that we hear of him. We are told that he drew large crowds, including the Emperor and other notables, when he played at the Benedictine Monastery at Ratisbon in 1471, and that his fame spread to many parts of Europe. He seems to have been organist at Nuremberg from 1446, but became resident at Munich in 1467. He visited various towns in 1450, and received many honours and gifts of money, including some from the Emperor Frederick III and the Duke of Ferrara, and was given a knighthood by the Pope.

He was fortunate in there being so excellent an organ at St. Sebald's, Nuremberg. It was built by Heinrich Traxeldorf in 1444 and cost 1150 gulden. It is said to have had an octave of pedals, and later stops to them, and probably possessed three manuals like the Halberstadt and later German organs, as well as 16 and 32 feet pipes. In 1479, an organ was built at Nuremberg with 1100 pipes

---

[1] A wind instrument with an enclosed reed.

for the great organ and 454 in the positive. We may be sure, then, that Paumann's organ was an extensive one.

Some 26 pieces and fragments from a Fundamentum by Paumann are to be found in the middle of the Buxheim Organ Book, otherwise the bulk of his organ compositions are those contained in his famous manuscript, the Fundamentum Organisandi (1452), which was found bound together with a collection of fifteenth-century songs known as the Locheim Song Book.

The Fundamentum Organisandi or 'the art of organizing', deals with the practice of writing upon a song or tenor by contrapuntal methods. Notes are treated in simple ascent (ascensus) or descent (descensus), first step by step as in the degrees of the scale, then by movement of thirds, fourths and fifths, over which a systematic descant is built. These are followed by short Pausae or single note Clausulae on the different degrees of the gamut (i.e. c to a). All were probably meant to be played, though the early ones are more in the nature of exercises. Later we reach more developed pieces built on definite tenors, such as 'En avois', 'Des Klaffers', 'Mit ganczem Willen', and works like the Magnificat on the 6th Tone, or that on the psalm verse 'Benedicite, Allmechtiger Got'. The arrangement of 'Allmechtiger Got' is an excellent example of the composition found in the Fundamentum. We get from it an impression comparable with that of an ornate 'Book of Hours' or other illuminated manuscript of the time.

Ex. XVI (Benedicite, Allmechtiger Got)

The Pausa on C has the effect of a Christmas carol, or of a winter scene as found in a fifteenth-century miniature, the whole suggesting the domestic simplicity of medieval Germany.

Ex. XVII (Pausa on C)

These pieces strike us as being definitely secular. In their peculiar way they are very melodious, and the characteristic flourishes and passage-work proclaim them as genuine keyboard pieces. They are well phrased, contrasted, and with fair variation. Basically they are composed in two parts, though the longer and more developed compositions are generally written with three voices.

Besides those of Paumann, there are also two compositions by composers named Paumgarten and Wilhelmus Legrant, which, together with three preambles, were apparently added at the end of the manuscript a few years later in 1455. Both pieces by the composers named are to be found again in the Buxheim Organ Book, with only slight alterations in the passage-work and accidentals. According to Sir John Stainer, Legrant (Le Grant) was in the Papal Choir in 1420.

It is the moment to discuss the general structure of medieval music, and organ compositions in particular. Basically the whole of medieval music was made by writing upon a pre-existing melody. This melody was usually allotted to the tenor part. The rhythm or note values of the original might be slightly altered. Above these notes, which were, more often than not, long-drawn-out, a second or third voice-part was added by way of decoration, which in turn became the proper melody of the piece. In the first part of Paumann's Fundamentum this method is illustrated by simple notes in the tenor, but in later examples the tenor is taken from some definite song, many of which are found in the prefixed Locheim Song Book. The musicians of the Middle Ages drew impartially from both sacred and secular sources, and the nature of the source had no particular bearing upon the purpose of the resulting composition. In the early Middle Ages the upper melodies were probably used as a melodic decoration, but by the time at which we have arrived the tenor became more and more of a fundamental bass. The material was now no longer taken always from an existing stock, and the part came to be constructed and used just like the bass of later music.

A melody was not always placed in the tenor, but was frequently employed in the descant or upper voice. In this case, it was often so altered or ornamented as to become a virtually new composition. In many instances of keyboard music whole pieces, both sacred and secular, were treated or arranged with ornamental elaboration, so that they became transcriptions comparable with much nineteenth-century piano music. The arrangement of vocal music for keyboard instruments was known as Intabulation (Intabolatura = putting into Tablature, i.e. for keyboards). When this form became ornate—which it was not always—it was said to be coloured (Coloratura). Various parts of the Mass were sometimes arranged for the organ. These compositions later became known as Organ Masses; and many portions of them were played in substitution for those particular sections of the Service. Most of the pieces in the Fundamentum Organisandi are of the tenor-melody type; but many in the Buxheim Organ Book are merely simple or elaborate intabulations. Of the other types of keyboard composition we must mention the Preamble—one of the most important things we have yet met with in instrumental history, for here we have the first instrumental prelude as such. These pieces probably originated in the organ Clausulae, and later became independent interludes. Of this more will be said later. Preambles are still compositions more or less based upon a tenor, but no pre-existent melody appears to have been used either in the upper or in the lower voice.

THE BUXHEIM ORGAN BOOK (c. 1460)

The Buxheim Organ Book is one of the most remarkable musical relics of the fifteenth century, containing as it does practically all—with the exception of the smaller Fundamentum of Paumann and a few other manuscripts—we know of the keyboard music of the later half of the fifteenth century. There are about 250 compositions of all types, ranging from about 1450 to 1470 in style. A few pieces are attributed to Paumann, Legrant, Paumgarten, Gotz, Spyra, Viletti, but the majority are anonymous sacred or secular song-arrangements. Many are in three parts, and are taken from the works of the early Burgundian composers such as Dufay and Binchois. Some, again, are in four-part writing. There are also three arrangements of what is presumed to be Dunstable's 'O Rosa Bella' (Nos. 39, 103 and 104). In about the middle of the manuscript, another 'Fundamentum' by Paumann, of a more elaborate nature, is placed. Here are given in short examples all the principles of writing or the different kinds of arrangements of a tenor, as in the previous work, together with some larger pieces. Apart from Paumann's compositions there are some on Magnificats, a complete Salve Regina, and an entire arrangement of the organ sections of the Mass, embracing 5 Kyries, a Gloria, a Credo, and a Sanctus. As opposed to the 'Fundamentum Organisandi', there are a number of preambles from the most elementary type to those of considerable technique.

By comparison with the 'Fundamentum Organisandi' these works are often more developed, though not so smooth or melodic as those of Paumann. Those that are attributed to him in the Buxheim manuscript such as the beautifully made 'Ich beger nit mer', stand out with even greater artistry, and it is possible that they represent a later development of his style than the 'Fundamentum'.

Ex. XVIII (Ich beger nit mer)

There is a certain dryness about Legrant's passage-work, though
the general movement is more progressive.

Ex. XIX (No. 113)

The piece by Gotz (No. 148) has a certain mournfulness of mood
as opposed to the smooth poetic quality of Paumann's music,
though the technique may be considered as more developed.

Ex. XX (No. 148)

Jacobus Viletti's piece 'Ein buer gein holtze', although the theme
has a German text, may be Italian—not only does the composer's
name suggest as much, but also the melodic style and characteristic duple measure—notwithstanding the simplicity of the

technique. Its charm and sweet simplicity of style cannot fail to attract us, once we have grasped its idiom.

Ex. XXI (Ein buer gein holtze)

Paumann's pieces stand out by reason of their sweetness and smoothness of phrase and poetic feeling, and may be the reason why in his day he was esteemed above his contemporaries. A final quotation from his 'Ich beger nit mer' will show the smooth melodic qualities of his art.

Ex. XXII

His is a world of unspoilt freshness yet to be appreciated by the latter-day musician.

THE PREAMBULA

One of the most interesting types in these early manuscripts from an instrumental point of view, is the Preambulum (Preamble), whose name speaks for itself (i.e. 'to preamble or prelude upon'). These pieces represent one of the earliest known forms of pure instrumental composition, and may be considered as the ancestors of all genuine keyboard music.

The simplest and no doubt the earliest examples consist of elementary passage-work over a ground note. They may be

regarded as an instrumental descant over an organal tenor, resem-
bling the organ clausula or the earlier church Organum Purum,
whence the preamble probably sprang. (See page 6-7.) In others,
more notes are spaced in the tenor, interlaced sometimes with
notes of other values to make three-part harmony by way of
variety. Such are found in the Buxheim Organ Book.

Ex. XXIII (No. 58)

The next growth has better accented passage-work, with a
more developed, though still characteristically medieval ground-
bass; and here we have, in however elementary a form, an individual and genuinely constructed keyboard piece. Though few preambles have great artistic value, some, particularly the more
developed ones, have an austere charm typical of fifteenth-century

Ex. XXIV (Preambulum on d)

music, and deserve more than bare respect as the beginnings of one
of the great branches of instrumental art, namely, keyboard
music. The preamble on *Re*, for instance, found in the last three
of the 'Fundamentum Organisandi' added in 1455, may be considered as one of the earliest instrumental preludes of the German
school. In its austerity it soars upwards, like the Gothic architec-
ture under which it was created, containing as it were the seeds of

D   B.K.M.

that forest whose tremendous ramifications we know in the pages of Bach and Beethoven.

The preamble on f (No. 234 Buxheim), after typical preluding in descant passage-work, followed by three-part note-against-note harmony, enters into a most appealing chorale-like tune in triple rhythm, which transports us into the atmosphere of fifteenth-century Germany with its homely medieval simplicity.

Ex. XXV (Preambulum on f. No. 234)

These compositions have a remarkable keyboard style, and for the period possess amazing variety. The typical turns and flourishes show that the executants must have had more than an elementary knowledge of keyboard technique.

SOME LATE FIFTEENTH-CENTURY ORGANISTS AND CLAVICHORDISTS

THE FIFTEENTH-CENTURY ORGAN

Our knowledge of the keyboard music of the next few years after the Buxheim Organ Book is imperfect. Names of organists are mentioned, such as Ruggio di Bor(g)ogna, organist at Bologna in 1474; Isaac Argyropoulos, engaged as organist by one of the Sforzas in 1472; Francesco d'Ana, 2nd organist of St. Mark's, Venice (1490–1503); Henry Abington of Lincoln (1418–1497); and the famous Heinrich Isaac, who was organist at Florence in 1485 after Squarcialupo. Winterfeld (1834) states, though possibly inaccurately, that Bartolomeo Battista was 1st organist at St. Mark's, Venice, in 1459, and we know that Bartolomeo Vielmis

PLATE III

A 15TH CENTURY CHORAL MASS WITH CONTEMPORARY
POSITIVE ORGAN IN UNCIAL
From the Prayer Book of Alfonso V of Aragon (1415-1458)

was 1st organist in 1490, Alvise Arciero, 2nd in 1503; but though nothing is known of their music, we can guess the type of compositions they played.[1] Pope Leo X (*c.* 1500) one of the most musically cultivated patrons of the time, declared that the best organists were Argyropoulos, Domenico the Venetian, and Daniel Stack.

The German school seems to have carried on its keyboard tradition, but nothing of importance is known until we come to the highly developed works of Arnolt Schlick (1512), and the more or less contemporary works of Paulus Hofhaimer and his associates.

Organ stops received names about this period, such as the Principal (Open 8 ft. diapason), Octave (Principal 4 ft), Quint (Twelfth 2,2/3 ft.), Super-Octave (Fifteenth 2 ft.), and Mixture stops like the Sesquialtera. Stopped pipes such as the Gedact (Stopped diapason) Bordun (Bourdon), and Klein Gedact (Flute), also seem to have been invented about this time, as well as certain Reeds like the Posaune (Trombone) and Trumpet, and stops akin to the Vox Humana. Later, stops having a string tone came on the scene. These afterwards received names like Violone and Viola da Gamba. The Spitzflöte, Gemshorn and Dolcan were also in vogue in the late fifteenth century. An organ at Sax, built in about 1490, had in the Hauptwerk: Principal, Octave, and a Mixture stop; a Rückpositiv an 8ve higher; and a Zinken in the Brustwerk. In an organ at Delft, the Hauptwerk possessed a Bourdon 16, Praestant 8, Mixture, and a Scharf, by about 1455. Probably many organs were larger than these, particularly in the greater German towns. Italian organs were somewhat different in registration, such as the one at St. Martin's at Lucca (*c.* 1480), where the manual apparently contained a Principal, Octave, 15th, and 22nd, and a Flute (4 ft.), with a Contrabass in the pedals. Those of cathedrals like Bologna and Venice had in the middle of the century something like a Principal 16 ft., Octave, 15th, 19th, 22nd,

---

[1] The keyboard music of Isaac is known, of course, as well as some Frottole of Francesco d'Ana (1504). There are also a number of Italian lute and other instrumental works of the period. *See p. 41.*

26th, 29th and a Flute; all of which agrees with their registration in the following century.[1]

The clavichordium or clavicymbalum had been in use throughout the fifteenth century. The earliest mention of a clavichord player of note is Pierre Beurse (late fifteenth century), followed by Henri Bredemero (1470–?), a well-known teacher and spinet player in the Low Countries.

[1] See Lunelli, R., 'Note sulle origini dell' organo italiano.' *Note archivio.* 1933. (Fasc. III.)

CHAPTER IV

EARLY SIXTEENTH-CENTURY ORGAN AND KEYBOARD MUSIC

LATE MEDIEVAL AND EARLY RENAISSANCE TENDENCIES

EARLY GERMAN
(a) ARNOLT SCHLICK (1460–1517?)

The first great master of the organ, and perhaps the greatest of his age, was Arnolt Schlick (1460– after 1517), organist of Heidelberg, who was one of the pioneers of that great organ school that found its culmination in Bach, for the intellectuality of his music and its austerity of style place him in the line of classical keyboard music, which ran through the names of Merulo, the two Gabrielis, Frescobaldi, Froberger and Buxtehude to the time of Bach.

Schlick's only real rival was the famous Paulus Hofhaimer (1459–1539). Unfortunately, we have only 14 organ works by Schlick, and although the actual Hofhaimer compositions are few and far between, there are a great many by his pupils; but despite the warmth and taste displayed in Hofhaimer's harmony, the general impression made by Schlick is one of austerity and nobility combined with a sweeping flow of movement and a spiritual level rising at moments to sublimity, e.g.

Ex. XXVI (Salve Regina)

37

In the 4th book of Ornithoparcus's 'Micrologus' (1517) he is addressed as 'the most attested of all', and the writer goes on: 'from your sentence no man will enter appeale, because there is no man either learneder or subtler in his art than your selfe. . . .' It seems that he made a tour as an organist towards the end of the fifteenth century, through Holland and Germany.

Schlick wrote two works, a 'Spiegel der Orgelmacher und Organisten' (The Mirror of Organists and Organ Builders) (1511), and a tablature of organ and lute music (1512). The first is a practical treatise on organ construction, dealing with the materials needed, the erection of the instrument, the tuning of pipes and so on. This is followed by a discussion on the important organs in existence, together with a few allusions to organ music and playing of the period. Mention is made of the difference of pitch in the manuals of an organ of that time—presumably as much as a 4th.[1] These generally extended to about three octaves with one or two manuals, having 8 or 9 stops for the first manual, three for the second or choir manual, the pedals three or four. The specification of Schlick's organ is generally reckoned to have run on these lines:

Hauptwerk	Rückpositiv
Principal (8 ft.) (large bore)	Principal (4 ft.)
Principal (8 ft.) (small bore)	Gemshorn (2 ft.)
Octave	Mixture
Mixture (16–18 ranks)	Zimbel
Gemshorn (4 ft.)	*Pedals*
Zimbel	Principal (16 ft.)
Regal	Octave (8 ft.)
Zink	Posaune (8 ft.)
Rauschpfeife	Mixture

The tablature (*Tabulaturen etlicher Lobgesang und Liedlein uff die Orgeln und Lauten*)[2] contains 14 organ pieces followed by 12 for lute

[1] See Kendall (Raymond), 'Notes on Arnolt Schlick', *Acta Musicologica*, XI, 1939.

[2] 'Tablatures of certain hymns of praise and small songs on the organs and lutes.'

and voice (some with 2 lutes accompanying), together with 3 pieces for lute alone. The works for organ are really early forms of chorale-preludes, and reach a more artistic whole than had previously been attained. Their form is noble and austere, and their intellectual style immediately places them in the front rank of organ music. They may well be called the first great keyboard music, and one day these fourteen compositions will be appreciated for what they are worth. The style adheres to the medieval tradition, though in a greatly developed form, for the technique is still that of working in descant upon a cantus-firmus, whether in the tenor or in the other voices. A few illustrations from his 'Salve Regina' and 'Maria Zart' will show the dignity and austerity of his art.

Ex. XXVII*a* (Salve Regina)

Ex. XXVII*b* (Maria Zart)

In the 'Maria Zart', as elsewhere, a genuine counter-melody is often given to the alto or tenor. This may help us in its interpretation; but a careful study of the parts will generally make the meaning of his music quite clear.

Schlick was much more medieval than Hofhaimer. The latter was deeply affected by the humanist movement, and was a man of the early German Renaissance. But Schlick's grandeur of conception and structural development sets him above that of Hofhaimer, in spite of the latter's warmth and richness of texture. Schlick was at Heidelberg while Hofhaimer was at Vienna, and Willi Apel's comparison of them with Bach and Handel is not inapt. Schlick's austerity of conception places him as a sort of late fifteenth-century Bach, while Hofhaimer's more open-hearted harmonies correspond to Handel's outlook. Schlick may one day be considered the greatest keyboard master of his time.

(b) Paulus Hofhaimer and his School. Leonhard Kleber

Paulus Hofheimer or Hofhaimer was born in 1459, apparently only a year before Schlick, but his music generally represents a later style. Nearly all his surviving works occur in the tablature books of his pupils and associates, who formed a school of composition basically like his own. Until recently, the Hofhaimer school was practically unknown but, thanks to Dr. H. J. Moser and others, a great deal of music has come to light in the form of the manuscript books of Kotter, Buchner and Sicher.

Hofhaimer's works, as we have them, range probably from about 1495 to 1520. Johann Kotter's (c. 1485–1541) tablature belongs to about 1513–35 and Hans Buchner's (1483–c. 1540) roughly to the same time, although it is dated at 1551. The next volumes representative of the German school are the better-known collections of Leonhard Kleber (1490–1556), which contain a vast body of compositions written between 1520 and 1525; and then the lesser-known tablature of Fridolin Sicher (1525),[1] who is thought to have studied with Hans Buchner.

[1] See Nef (W. R.), *Der St Galler Organist Fridolin Sicher und seine Orgeltabulatur* (Basel). 1938.

PLATE IV

PAULUS HOFHAIMER (1459–c.1539)
From the drawing by Albrecht Dürer

Paulus Hofhaimer had close associations with Heinrich Isaac, organist at Florence and founder of the German branch of the Flemish school. Around Isaac there formed an intimate circle, including Hofhaimer, Senfl (Martin Luther's friend) and Heinrich Finck, and here much was done to foster a German school and to encourage the more direct form of harmony that came into vogue in sympathy with the Lutheran movement. Not only religious reform, but also the stimulating impressions made by the humanistic movement affected the keyboard music of this school.

Whether Heinrich Isaac (*c.* 1450–1517) had an initial influence on this organ school is difficult to tell. His few keyboard (organ?) pieces are quite early in style, though they occur in tablatures much later than his period (i.e. Fridolin Sicher, St. Gallen 530). Here is an example of one marked 'Isaac composuit'.

Ex. XXVIII

(Maria Junckfraw hoch geborn)

(St. Gallen 530 fol. 92 r.)

Hofhaimer spent some time as organist to the Archduke Sigismund of Tyrol (*c.* 1480–1490), and in the court orchestra of Frederick III at Graz; but the greater part of his life was passed at the sumptuous court of the Emperor Maximilian I (1480–1519), where he was not only the organist but a musician much beloved of the Emperor himself. While playing the organ at St. Stephen's, Vienna, in the presence of three crowned heads, Hofhaimer, at the request of the Emperor, was made a Knight of the Golden Spur by King Ladislaus of Hungary. An old poem states that:

> *He played the organ with might*
> *And with main,*
> *Like a thousand voices at once,*
> *Like the rush of chariots.*

Ottomar Luscinus (Nachtgall) said that his playing was 'full of warmth and power, uniting most wonderful finger-skill with a majestic flow of harmony previously unsurpassed.' Beyond the warm atmosphere of the Viennese Court,[1] where he attracted many pupils and admirers, it seems his influence, in common with the general humanistic tendencies of his surroundings, spread out as far as Switzerland.

After Maximilian's death in 1519 he retired to Salzburg, where he became organist to the Archbishop. Here he seems to have remained until his death, the supposed date of which is 1539. There is an interesting set of engravings of a procession,[2] in which a number of musicians are seen drawn through the streets on decorated waggons. On one of these is seen Hofhaimer, seated at an organ. It is a fairly large (positive) instrument, and is being blown at the back by bellows. There is also a report of a portrait by Lucas Cranach, but the best that has survived is undoubtedly the one by Albrecht Dürer, reproduced in this book facing p. 40.

Hofhaimer's compositions are well described as 'warmth of harmony', and all his school are characterized by richness of texture, though many of them border on sameness. Luscinus was also right in describing his harmony as 'a majestic flow previously unsurpassed'. Most pre-Hofhaimer keyboard harmony was either austere, or based on the bare fifth, like that of the Buxheim Book. Hofhaimer's harmony is warmer and superior in its spacing and arrangement, and produces an effect akin to the later German schools (e.g. O Dulcis Maria).

Ex. XXIX (O Dulcis Maria)

(St. Gallen 530)

[1] The ducal court was at Innsbruck.
[2] *The Triumph of Maximilian* (Hans Burgkmair).

Hofhaimer's school may be called Viennese, though many of his pupils resided and worked in Germany and Switzerland (e.g. Kotter). Their expressiveness and texture were characteristic of the city where Hofhaimer dwelt. The music of Buchner, Kotter and others is akin to their master's, though not always woven with such grace and artistry. In form and structure, however, these men were often more developed than Hofhaimer, and we see the factor of free fugal imitation beginning to come into vogue.

Ex. XXX (In dulci jubilo. Anon. St, Gallen 530)

Buchner's works are fully representative of the Hofhaimer style. The poem already mentioned speaks of him as 'skilfully playing four etherial voices together'. His 'Fundamentum' (c. 1513–1535) is in three parts. An introduction on notation and fingering is followed by compositions on cantus-firmus tenors, and others in free contrapuntal style. Kotter's tablature is in two parts, copied presumably for Bonifacius Ammerbach of Basel. This may originally have been intended for the clavichord, to judge from the style and the fact that Bonifacius was a clavichord player.[1] Beside the usual works on canti-firmi, ornamental song arrangements and some preambles—forms that are still in existence in a more developed style—there are seven early German dances,[2] that go further to show that the work was intended for the clavichord.[3] The examples given by Apel show a series of well-wrought and, at times, richly woven compositions.

[1] In a later catalogue of his library, one of the books is labelled 'pro clavicordio'.

[2] See also Merian (W), Der Tanz, 1927 (Sammelbände der Inter. Musikgesellschaft) and Halbig (H), Klaviertanz.

[3] Willi Apel. The Musical Quarterly, New York, 1937. (Early German Keyboard Music.) See, however, p. 117, footnote 1, for contrary view.

In general character, however, these keyboard works are
limited. They have not Arnolt Schlick's wide outlook and spiritual conception, though a certain warmth and interest of texture
give them an important position in the history of keyboard music,
and many deserve to be brought into our normal organ repertory.

Leonhard Kleber's (1490–1556) manuscript volumes (1520–25)
represent a large contribution to the later productions of the early
German schools. They are solidly built with a modern conception
of harmony and a definite instrumental sense, the chords and passages moving with the true keyboard feeling.

Ex. XXXIa (Preambulum on C)

Ex. XXXIb (Preambulum on d)

Kleber indeed contributed a great deal in the advance of organ
music, and many of his compositions are excellent works. We find
preambles, fantasias and compositions entitled 'finales', composed
on secular or sacred themes.

He is spoken of as the first of the 'colourists', and it is true that
his music abounds in the typical and endless 'turns' that became
habitual with the colourists of a later date. Among them this
developed into a mechanical form of counterpoint, but Kleber's
passage-work is woven with true artistic feeling. His work may be
counted as almost the last compositions of the old German school
of organ playing.

PLATE V

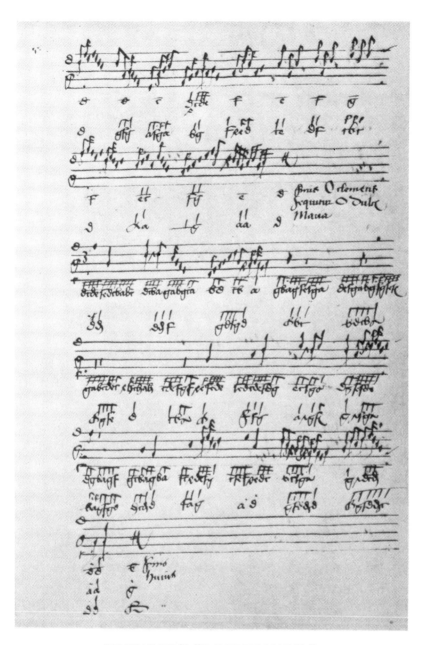

HOFHAIMER'S "O DULCIS MARIA"
From an old German Tablature

CONTEMPORARIES. FRENCH AND ENGLISH KEYBOARD MUSIC

There are many names of organists recorded of this period. Conrad V. Speyer (?–1526), active organist in 1513; Ottomar Luscinus (Nachtgall) (1480–1537); Zuane di Maria, 1st organist at St. Mark's, Venice, in 1502, whom some esteemed as the first organ composer of his day; Dionisio Memo, 1st organist at St. Mark's (1507), who was persuaded by Henry VIII to come to England as a resident organist in 1516; and Marco Antonio di Bologna, now known as the elder Cavazzoni. Of the early Italian school, however, we shall speak later.

In France we find the Attaignant collection, consisting mostly of songs, dances and motet arrangements for organ, spinet or clavichord. There are 3 sets of Chansons Musicales for 'Orgues, Espinettes, Manicordions' . . . etc. (1530); Quatorze Galliards (1530); a 'Tablature pour le jeu d'Orgues, Espinettes et Mani-cordions' (1531), and a 'Magnificat sur les huit tons' (1531). The compositions on sacred canti-firmi are not of great importance. They are rather conventional though not without artistry. (See Rokseth's transcription of Attaignant's 1531 edition.) e.g.

Ex. XXXII (Credo 'Patrem')

Many of the dances, however, are particularly attractive. There is a distinct modern feeling about them, as in the following:

Ex. XXXIII (Gaillarde)

Representing this period in England are the organ pieces of John Redford (*c.* 1485–1545), the organist of old St. Paul's. His works are probably quite early, and are at present very little known.[1] They are austere and somewhat rigid, yet not without a sense of dignity. In style they may almost be considered Flemish, though the Flemish influence was probably early since the English organists seem to have formed a school of their own by the end of the first half of the century. e.g.

Ex. XXXIV (Lucem Tuam)

Ex. XXXV (A Meane)

John Taverner's (*c.* 1495–1545) organ pieces may also be considered as of this period.

LATER GERMAN SCHOOLS

The German school continued with the colourist movement until about 1600. It was superseded then by a new German school arising from another source, and it was this that led to the music of Bach and his associates. The most important of the colourist composers were Jacob Paix (fl. 1570), Woltz (fl. 1580–90), and above all Nicholas Ammerbach (1530–1597). Ammerbach's tablature *Orgel oder Instrument Tabulatur* came out in 1571; it contains

[1] See Margaret Glyn, *Early English Organ Music*, 1934, and particularly C. F. Pfatteicher, *John Redford*, 1934.

points of interest with which we shall deal later. As well as transcriptions of famous Italian composers—'coloured' (interwoven in florid polyphony) or otherwise (simple counterpoint)—Ammerbach included a great number of German dances, passemezzi, and other dance pieces, many of which are of excellent quality. Paix's organ tablature came out in 1583, and Woltz's in 1617 (*Nova Musices Organicae Tabulatura*). Some excellent dance pieces, again, are to be found in Augustus Normiger's '*Tabulaturbuch auff dem Instrumente*' (1598).

Good though much of this music is in its way, the composers have neither the fire nor the imagination of the contemporary Italians, nor their technical advancement. Thus they have never come to the foreground as compared with the Spanish and English. It is true that very few of their works have been published, and possibly we may one day find more value in them than has hitherto been conceded.

PART II

THE RENAISSANCE

Chapter V

SIXTEENTH-CENTURY ITALY

The Renaissance of Music. Venice

The greatest event in the musical history of this time was the formation of famous Italian schools under the direct influence of Flemish composers, at Rome, Ferrara, Florence, Brescia, Mantua and—of particular importance—at Venice, where much of the foundation of instrumental music was laid.

Since about 1430, Flemish musicians had freely visited Italy and had impressed their methods upon the practice of music there, which appeared to be rather secular, as we gather from such frottolas and villanelles by Tromboncino and others published at the beginning of the century (1504). The only possible Italian organ composer in the Buxheim Book is Jacobus Viletti, whose contribution is somewhat secular in nature. Not until about 1500 did anything like a true Italian school of organ composition develop.[1]

The Italian cities differed from the still medieval towns of Germany. In that more luxurious climate it was the time of the high Renaissance, and Italy had already for generations been a very fountain of creative art. It was only natural that a music imbued with the Renaissance spirit should arise there.

Greatly to the assistance of Italian organ composers was the simplified method of writing for the keyboard, as opposed to the clumsy German tablature. This was also encouraged by the famous Venetian firm of Petrucci and others, which from 1498 printed all sorts of music, including works by most of the famous Flemish composers. Venice was at the apogee of her wealth and glory. The focus of the new school was St. Mark's. That cathedral had for many years encouraged organs and organ playing. In 1318 Zucchetti built and played on an organ there, and there is no reason

---

[1] As far, at least, as surviving evidence goes to show.

to suppose this to have been the first. The organ contest between Landini and Pesaro probably took place there in 1364. In 1389 a second organ was built, and from that time the tradition of 1st and 2nd organist was maintained until the end of the Venetian school. Pedals were introduced about 1470.[1]

The idea of placing two organs in opposite galleries probably came, like the architectural style of this church, from Constantinople. Antiphonal singing, which was predominant at St. Mark's, may also be of Byzantine source.

The Instrumental Forms of the Italian Renaissance

The Ricercar and Fantasia

A word here may be said about Italian instrumental compositions as a whole. The early German school had largely employed the technique of writing compositions upon the tenor, as in medieval times. Whether the original tune was placed in some form or other in the tenor voice, or whether it was decorated as a descant melody above it, the basic idea was still that of writing upon another melody. The Italian style derived from Flanders, where polyphony of a different form had been greatly cultivated. Instead of decorating a tenor with the imposition of different patterns or rhythms, a single theme or phrase was developed by repetitions or answers with that same phrase, above or below the original theme, at an interval of a 4th, 5th or 8ve, while it was still in progress, in a series of overlapping utterances. Such fugal polyphony, which we are apt to think of as the outcome only of a high European civilization, has, in point of fact, been observed in a primitive form in remote Polynesia. It may have originated in antiphonal choral singing, which we know was practised by the Hebrews, Syrians, Byzantines, and possibly by the Egyptians. In Europe it occurs in the early fourteenth century in forms like the rota, rondellus, and the French and Italian caccia. By the middle of the fifteenth century Flemish composers had developed this art of answering voice by voice in harmonious overlapping sequence by

[1] Presumably by Bernard, the German organist at St. Mark's.

certain principles. A theme was not only combined with its exact replica, the latter entering with a certain delay—this being what we now know simply as 'canon'—but also the theme was cunningly varied so as to form another, yet reminiscent theme, to be worked into the general pattern. The Flemings devoted intensive study to this art, which they applied to the motet and the various sections of the Mass. Flemish composers, attracted to Italy by the wealth and splendour of the Renaissance, brought this technique to play upon Italian music.

(1) Ex. XXXVI–VII (Ricercare a tre)

(1) a = theme, m = motive, v = varied, Aug = augmented, dim = diminished.

Ex. XXXVII

When this style was imposed upon the lyrical part-song there resulted the polyphonic chanson and its like. Developed in its full complexity in non-versified types of composition and in works for instruments, it became known as the 'Ricercare' or 'Ricercar'. The term implies a searching out—searching out of a theme buried in contrapuntal devices such as proportional rhythms, florid additions, inversions, contrary motion, augmentations, diminutions and so on. In instrumental, particularly keyboard compositions, where each voice had a chance of developing at length, the ricercar was a vehicle of the finest artistry. It was looked upon as the highest of musical forms. Let us take an example by Adrian Willaert (1480–1562) which, although only in three simple voice-parts, is of great structural complexity. It is written for three instruments and probably represents an early form of the Italian ricercar. (See Ex. XXXVI and Ex. XXXVII.)

Note how closely the themes are dovetailed, and that each apparently new theme is derived from the initial one. Even the remote ones like

Ex. XXXVIII

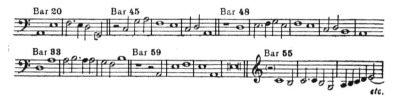

may have been suggested by the original subject. In more complex examples analysis is often difficult. Three or four secondary motives, either new or derived from one other, may be worked into the pattern. In the more developed pieces one often finds things of great beauty.

Ex. XXXIX (Ricercare No. 9) (Frescobaldi)

The cousin of the ricercar, the fantasia, was a similar composition with a greater freedom, as the name implies, for invention in the parts. It was a highly evolved composition, but less rigid and compact in its contrapuntal developments. In later instances, it was often constructed in different sections, in which the theme took on a different form in another series of entries or 'exposition'.

Other compositions, worked on hymns, Magnificats and the different parts of the Mass and other services, were even freer, but were still based on contrapuntal devices. Many instrumental works of the period, such as the lute and organ music, were transcriptions of vocal compositions. It must not, however, be taken that the early organists merely copied vocal music or a vocal style, as was once believed. They practised an artistic and instrumental weaving of the parts, from, or over, the original theme. Sometimes the theme was placed in the bass, sometimes in the treble, or used in combination with the bass theme in diminution.

These fantasias and ricercari may at a casual glance seem severe; but that is because we are too familiar with the variety of modern harmony, and do not take enough care with the subtle phraseology of this early counterpoint which, if examined closely, will disclose the greatest interest and variety. From these closely knit forms the modern fugue took its shape as the subjects or themes became more highly characterized, the composition as a whole becoming more monothematic, the old secondary subjects falling into place as proper countersubjects. Of the later forms and other Italian types, like the canzon and toccata, we shall speak again.

Early Italian Organ Music

The early phase of the Venetian organ school, or indeed that of Italian music as a whole, is difficult to descry. Zuana-di-Maria had a great reputation as an organ composer, and we hear that when Giustiniani's secretary was commanded to play before Henry VIII in 1515, he asked for some of Maria's compositions to be sent to him. We of to-day know, so far, only some vocal works—frottolas, etc. (Petrucci, 1504).

Dionisio Memo, a presumed pupil of both Maria and Hofhaimer, was 1st organist at St. Mark's in 1507. He played the organ for Henry VIII before a host of virtuosi and musicians, in 1516, on an instrument which he is said to have brought with him 'at great care and cost' from Venice. Henry VIII insisted upon the French Ambassadors listening to his music for four hours.

The first keyboard work recorded in Italy is a set of frottolas arranged for organ—'Frotole Intabulate da Sonare per Organi', Lib. 1 (Rome) 1517—copies of which are listed as being in the library of Count von Nostitz-Rieneck near Prague, and in the Columbia (Chapter) Library at Seville. The work in the latter library cannot be traced, only an eleventh volume of frottolas existing. According to authorities the only known copy is in the library of the Marchese Polesini, Parenzo, Italy.[1]

MARCO ANTONIO DI BOLOGNA

The next record of Italian organ music is in the little known 'Recerchari, Motetti, Canzoni' of Marco Antonio di Bologna (1523), now identified as the elder Cavazzoni. There is apparently only one copy in existence.[2] It is of particular interest as showing the already developed state of Italian organ music at Venice before the influence of Adrian Willaert and his school was felt. These have often been considered the pioneers of Italian instrumental art, in spite of the fact that lute music had been in print since 1507, and works suitable or written for consorts of instruments were in vogue from at least 1535. Bologna's little volume of organ pieces consists of 2 ricercari alternated by 2 motet arrangements, followed by four keyboard transcriptions of French songs, called 'Canzoni'. They are built on the lines of the 'chanson', and show one of the earliest uses of formal repetitions in keyboard music. The arrangement of 'Madame, vous aves mon coeur', for instance, has an initial section which contains a definite contrasting subject.

[1] See Jeppesen. *Die Italianische Orgelmusik am Anfang des Cinquecento* (Copenhagen), Munksgaard, 1943.
[2] British Museum.

Ex. XL (Madame, vous aves mon cœur)

Antonio di Bologna

(Brit.Mus.)

This is repeated in another form 6 bars later, followed by further repetitions, modifications and extensions of the original section. At bar 44 a modified version of the first subject of 5 bars is repeated intact, after which there is a complete recapitulation of the first 20 bars of the piece, to be followed, with the interspersion of a small bridge, by a coda of 5 almost similarly repeated bars, which brings the composition to a satisfactory close. It is too long to quote in full, but it may roughly be described as: ab, a', b', a², a³, a³, ab', c, c'. It is a composition fraught with a systematic formal sense, and at the same time an emotional intensity that speaks of the Renaissance spirit in its fullness in Italian organ music. In one canzone a portion of the initial theme is repeated three times.

Baldassare da Imola was 2nd organist of St. Mark's from 1533 to 1541, where he was succeeded by Buus, but nothing is known about his life or works. The same must be said of the 1st organist, Fra Giovanni Armonio (c. 1516–1552).

THE FIRST VENETIAN SCHOOL

(a) ADRIAN WILLAERT

Adrian Willaert (1480–1562) went to Venice in 1527, and was appointed musical director (Maestro di cappella) at St. Mark's. No doubt he was an organist as well as a composer. He is supposed to have been a pupil of Josquin and of Mouton whom he had met in Paris. So great was his reputation that he has been commonly thought of as the founder of the Venetian school. His genius warrants our considering him, at any rate, as the chief influence. Venice delighted to honour him, and the citizens called his music 'drinkable gold'—Aurum Potabile. Some of his fame rests on his having been one of the first to compose for two separate choirs (see p. 94). He was a man of wide outlook and was probably instrumental in laying down the foundation of tonic and dominant harmony. Twice he went back to his native country, in 1542 and 1556, but he died at Venice in 1562. An interesting account of a painting by an artist named Harman is given by a contemporary of his. It was an illustration of a musical performance at the Ducal Palace and there Willaert was depicted playing a small organ surrounded by singing monks, while an aristocratic audience of men and women listened in the background. Great as was his own effort as an artist, he had equal influence through his disciples, many of whom were to carry on and mature the Venetian school in the next generation. Such were Jachet Buus, Cipriano de Rore, Cavazzoni, Parabosco, and Andrea Gabrieli. No organ compositions by Willaert exist, but 8 instrumental ricercari in three parts came out in Tiburtino's 'Fantasie et Recerchari' (1549), and 9 more of his ricercari are in his 'Fantasie, Recercari' . . . of 1559. These, though, had probably been composed at an earlier date.

(b) JACHET BUUS

Jachet Buus (1505–1564) was 2nd organist in 1541. His first volume, 'Recercari . . . da cantare e sonare d'organo e altri stromenti' written on four staves, came out in 1547, to be followed by

'Il Secondo Libro di Recercari', in 1549. Both were conceivably composed after Willaert's, he having probably been a pupil or disciple. Buus's second book of Ricercari (1549) is also written on staves, 'apt' as it may be said 'for either instruments or voices'. But another volume, also in the British Museum, containing the whole with ornamental arrangements written as a series of organ ricercari, shows how they normally transcribed vocal works for keyboard instruments. It is entitled 'Intabolatura d'Organo di Recercari' (1549). Buus's works have only sparingly been transcribed.[1] I therefore quote the beginning of one of his ricercari, if only for the sake of comparison with later types of compositions. (Note entrance and variants of the theme.)

Ex. XLI (Ricercare No. 3)

The ricercari and fantasias of Willaert and others of this date are severe, close-knit and at first difficult to follow. From an aesthetic point of view they have a great richness and dignity, like the colour of old gold. Study gradually reveals the meaning and beauty of these compositions. In their time they were highly esteemed,

[1] See Sunderland (G), 'The Ricercari of Jacques Buus.' *Musical Quarterly*, (N.Y.), Oct., 1945.

although often thought too long as voluntaries at divine service—so much we gather from Doni's remark that 'a bell was sometimes rung to stop the organists with their long ricercari'. All these forms, including the latter toccatas and canzoni, served as embellishments of the service, as well as for secular and domestic purposes.

Girolamo Cavazzoni (The Younger) of Urbino

An important composer of that time, and of comparatively recent discovery, is Girolamo Cavazzoni. He published two versatile volumes as early as 1542–3, but, like Buus, he represents a style later than Willaert's. Little is known of his life beyond that he came from Urbino.

His 'Intavolatura' in two volumes (1542–43) is a varied collection of ricercari, canzoni, contrapuntal settings of hymns, and some organ arrangements of 3 Masses and 4 Magnificats. The arrangement of the different portions of the Mass forms an early example of the Italian Organ-Mass, in which each section is made into an new ornate composition on its own, and was obviously used as a substitute for that portion. The ricercari are slightly longer and show great contrapuntal ingenuity, as do the Magnificats, in which the initial subject is often interwoven with cunning variations and diminutions. The canzoni are rather lighter in texture and contrast. The hymn arrangements make particularly attractive pieces, as in the following. (See Ex. XLII.)

Cavazzoni's style is rich and dignified, though at times somewhat stolid. His counterpoint is characterized by a close interlocking of parts and a consistent legato; yet within this distinct limitation he obtains a great variety. Occasionally, as in the last two ricercari, a 3/2 section is inserted in a common-time work, as in the later Italian canzon. Passage-work is only sparely resorted to and then rather formally. Interwoven counterpoint is the chief characteristic. This, although severe, has a nobility which conveys the magnificence of sixteenth-century Italy. There are also many compositions—among the hymns, for instance—which are quite pleasing in character, and warmer and more interesting than

Ex. XLII (Lucis Creator Optime)

Buus's or Willaert's. Cavazzoni is unknown to-day except to historians. Further study of the first half of the sixteenth century will probably establish his reputation among the finest organ composers of that age.

THE SPANISH SCHOOL. ANTONIO CABEZÓN

Another important field of keyboard music in which Flemish influence played a part was the Spanish school of the first half of the sixteenth century. Very prolific and as important as anything in Europe, outside Italy, it produced lute music at quite an early date, and later viol, organ and other keyboard compositions, as well as a vast mass of liturgical music. In spite, however, of many original and, indeed, extremely advanced ideas, the Spaniards never throughout the century attained the precedence of the Italians' art.

Many lute pieces by Luis Milan (*d.* 1561) and others are both attractive and modern in style. They are generally lighter and more pleasing than the average instrumental compositions of other schools. The keyboard works of Bermudo (*b.* 1510) and

Tomas de Santa Maria (*d.* 1570) too, are excellent compositions, and things of beauty, although falling somewhat short of the artistry and sublimity of the best of the Italian work. Venegas de Henestrosa should also be mentioned, who published a 'Libro de Cipra Nueva Para Tecla, Harpa y Vihuela' in 1557 containing keyboard and other works of famous Spanish composers. At a later date there was a Seb. Aguilera de Heredia (*b.* 1570), organist at Saragossa in 1603.

The greatest of Spanish keyboard composers was undoubtedly Antonio Cabezón (1510–1566), organist to Philip II, whom he attended on his journeys to Flanders and Luxemburg in 1548–1551, when it is known he visited England. The greatest organist in Spain, he was also among the best harpsichord players of his time. By Philip II's orders his keyboard and other works were published by his son in 1577, eleven years after his death. His work is divided into various sections, containing compositions in 2, 3 and 4 voices, apparently intended for all keyboard or alternative instruments like the guitar (vihuela) and other instruments. Later there are 'Versi' (verses), 'Intermedos', 'Tientos' (a simpler form of ricercar or fantasia) and pieces on themes by Josquin, Buus, Willaert and Clemens-non-Papa.

Most remarkable and most modern in Cabezón—as also in the lute music of Narvaez (1538) and Mudarra (1546)—is the form of variation 'diferencia' or 'glosa', used when working on a theme. A different harmony or texture was employed on the re-entrance of a melody, and it is often thought that they influenced the English and Netherlandish composers, and possibly the Italians (Neapolitans and Romans)—Frescobaldi for instance—in their instrumental variations of the following age. More of this, however, later.

Most of Cabezón's compositions are written in the dignified style of the ricercar. These pieces are well constructed and are full of invention and daring. Harmonically he stretched to the limits of his day, venturing to the point of chromaticism. The variety in the vast bulk of his work is amazing, and a kind of directness in his phrasing stamps him as one of the most advanced keyboard

composers of the period. His chromaticisms express a peculiarly
Spanish melancholy, apart from his genius for colour.

Ex. XLIII (Intermedio No. 4, 'Rex Virginum')

His sense of grandeur may be illustrated by the harmonically conceived climax at the end of a Tiento on the 2nd Tone:

Ex. XLIV (Tiento on the 2nd tone)

His method in constructing a series of variants or 'glosas' on a
theme is worthy of illustration, affording as it does an excellent
example of the early use of the variation form:

PLATE VI

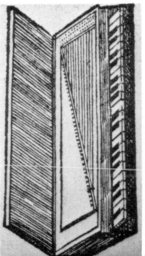

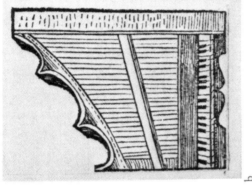

WOODCUT ILLUSTRATIONS OF EARLY 16TH CENTURY KEYBOARD INSTRUMENTS

a. Clavichord   *b.* Clavicitherium   *c.* Virginal

(These illustrations have been used by various early writers on instruments)

d. DRAWING OF POSITIVE ORGAN USED AT BRUSSELS IN 1490

Ex. XLV (Fabordon and Variation on the 8th tone)

The passage-work is flowing and well conceived, and shows that he must have had a developed technique. He was indeed the fore-father of much that was to come in keyboard writing. His influ-ence may well have extended farther than we can tell by direct evidence. Certain it is that Cabezón was, outside the Venetian school, amongst the greatest of the keyboard composers of the first half of the sixteenth century.

Chapter VI

THE SECOND VENETIAN SCHOOL

After the age of Willaert, Buus and Cavazzoni, which ended about 1560, Venetian music bloomed into a second and more developed period. The first was rich but rather severe. The flowering of the second reached a glory comparable with the Roman school of Palestrina. In invention of form, power of expression and richness of colour it was without parallel in Europe. Venice had been a cradle of instrumental music, and it was there that keyboard music developed into forms destined to influence the traditions of classical music.

The rich intellectual life of the great city was reflected in its music—and let us remember that it was the scene of the creations of Titian, Tintoretto and Paul Veronese. Venice was a city of pomp and splendour. She was called 'The Queen of the Sea', and life there was coloured by all manner of Levantine contacts and the adventures of her merchants and soldiers. All this probably affected Venetian music. After the defeat of the Turks at Lepanto (1571) the republic enjoyed a period of comparative peace and security, and this may have played no small part in the musical developments that took place about this time. An indication of the attractiveness of Venetian musical life is provided by Thomas Coryat's remark in his 'Crudities' (1608) on the concerts he had attended there: 'I heard the best musick that ever I did in all my life . . . so good that I would willingly goe a hundred miles a foote at any time to heare the like.' And later he says that the music was 'so good, so delectable, so rare, so superexcellent . . . that it did even ravish and stupifie all the strangers that never heard the like.' When Orlandus Lassus desired instrumentalists and singers of the best quality for the chapel at Munich, he went to Venice to procure them. We recall Ruskin's description of the city as a place of 'crimson fretted with gold'. As a finish we may add Fynes Moryson's account of the music of Venice from the unpublished chapters of his 'Itinerary' (*c.* 1617): 'to which studyes I will add the Art of Musick, wherein the Italians, and espetially the Venetians have in all types excelled, and most at this day, not in light tunnes and hard striking of the stringe (which they dislike), nor in companyes of wandering fidlers (whereof they have none or very fewe single men of small skill) but in Consortes of grave solome Musicke, sometymes running so sweetly with soft touching of the strings, as may seeme to ravish the hearers spiritt from his body, which musike they use at many private and publike meetings, but espetially in their Churches, where they joyne with it winde Instruments, and most pleasant voices of boyes and men, being indeed such Musicke as cannot but stir up devotion in the hearers. . . . the Popes Chappell hath no instruments of musicke, but only most excellent voyces of men and boyes.' (C. Hughes. *Shakespeare's Europe. The Unpublished Chapters of Fynes Moryson.* 1903.)

TYPES OF COMPOSITION

The keyboard compositions of this period, beyond the usual arrangements of motets, etc., were almost exclusively in three forms, the Ricercare, the Canzone and the Toccata.

The Ricercare or Ricercar, the oldest of the three, has already been described as the predecessor of the instrumental fugue. Its subject, usually simple, was worked out in close polyphonic fashion with all manner of contrapuntal devices, but without the variety and cumulative development of the more advanced fugue. Even at the end of the sixteenth century the ricercar was still considered the highest form of instrumental art. It was serious in nature, and although becoming freer as time went on, with a growing tendency towards monothematicism—e.g. the 'Ricercar on the 10th tone' by Giovanni Gabrieli—they generally maintained their strict style.

The Canzone or Canzon (later Canzona) had its origin in the part-songs of early France and Italy. It may be described as something played that had originally been sung. The 'Canzone alla Francese', 'Canzone a Francese', or 'Canzone Francese', is a free form of composition based on the rhythmic patterns of early song-forms, with contrasts of texture and mood. As the name implies, its origin was the early French chanson. The voice-parts were written mainly in the same metre, and thus was laid the basis of the homophonic harmony of later usage. The rhythm, with certain variations, ran as follows:

Ex. XLVI

Such simplicity and direct appeal became very popular in the sixteenth century. The instrumental canzone was an instrumental adaption of that rhythm. Canzoni were from first to last based on this pattern, even though we may get such examples as this:

Ex. XLVII

The refrain or ritornello of the early part-songs was useful in making for contrast and a change of phraseology. In the instrumental canzoni of the Gabrielis, as we shall see, this was carried to great effect. In the keyboard canzoni ornamentation was frequently employed. The canzon in many ways was a forerunner of the later sonata, its theme being not only more predominant, but used in frequent imitation. It is lighter than the ricercar and not so contrapuntal, e.g.

Ex. XLVIII (Canzon No. 1. Sacrae Symphoniae. 1597)

The Toccata is the source of a musical style belonging peculiarly to the keyboard. What the ricercar is to the fugue and the canzon to the sonata, the toccata is to the instrumental prelude and similar compositions. Although passage-work predominates in the six-teenth-century toccata it is not really of a bravura character. The essence of it is a style arising from the nature of keyboard instru-ments. No doubt something was contributed to the toccata by the 'tastar de corde', a simple lute piece designed for 'trying out' or testing one's instrument (tastar = to touch, and hence to test) and for preparing an audience for something more positive to come—a prelude, in fact. Such pieces were at first a mere string of chords followed by rather insignificant scale passages such as we get in Dalza's Intabolatura (1508). The word 'toccata' probably comes from 'toccare' (= to touch, to knock, or even to beat, i.e. the drums). From the application of 'toccare' to the playing even of percussion instruments a toccata might imitate the fanfare of an instrumental band, or denote the fanfare itself. Monteverdi used the word 'toccata' for the trumpet fanfare in his opera 'Orfeo'. As a significant keyboard composition, however, it did not become predominant until about the middle of the century.

The sixteenth-century toccata was by no means formless. After a frequently brief introduction, there comes a flow of quavers and semiquavers distributed between the hands, accompanied by chords. This continues with often increased complexity until we come to a new section—usually a kind of slow fugue or ricercar, written mostly in crotchets and quavers. No change of tempo is indicated; but we get the impression of a slower movement and the introduction of a more serious character into the piece. The semiquaver movement is then resumed. This gives a sort of A, B, A, form, which is even more premonitory of the sonata than is the canzon. There is, however, a shorter type, in which the middle section is diminished or even missing altogether.

The technique and passage-work of the toccata may be left until we come to Merulo, a great master of this form. The toccata developed further at the hands of Frescobaldi and Froberger, and has remained an independent form of composition down to modern times. By the middle of the seventeenth century, how-ever, its predominance as a type began to diminish in favour of forms like the Suite and Sonata. The sixteenth-century toccata, like the ricercar and canzon, served both for ecclesiastical and mundane occasions.

For the moment we shall not speak of types of composition that were to be more characteristic of the early part of the seventeenth century.

Remarkable in the music of the sixteenth century is the richness of harmony, as well as the development of form and technique. More passing-notes and inversions are used, though basically the harmonic resources remain the same, chromatic and dissonant harmony being as yet little known. The use of suspensions, however, is developed to the highest degree, and much of the richness of the music is obtained thereby.

The Sixteenth-Century Organ

We have seen that St. Mark's possessed traditionally two organs and maintained, from the fifteenth century at least, a 1st and a 2nd organist. The instruments were opposite each other, over the two musicians' galleries, and appear to have accompanied antiphonal choirs. Little is known about them, beyond that they possessed 126 keys by 1561. According to Antegnati, Italian organs were not so large as those of Germany and Spain, though their tone was sweeter and their action smoother.[1]

Thus the organ of St. Maria at Dantzig (1585) possessed 55 stops. The 'Great' contained 13, the Front choir 8, the Rückpositive (Back Positive) 18, the pedals 4, together with 12 stops by the side of the pedals, for the Great organ.

The organ at Halle, built presumably in 1500 and still in working order in 1712, contained before 1600 at least:

Oberwerk (Great)

1. Principal (8 ft. on Manual) (16 ft. on Pedal)
2. Octava (Manual 4 ft.)
3. Mixtur (Manual and Pedal)
4. Zimbel (Manual and Pedal)
5. Nachthorn (4 ft.)
6. Querpfeiff (8 ft.)

[1] The organ of our own time is normally too powerful for the 'sweet and smooth' compositions of the Venetian organists.

On same Manual but in front

7. Principal (2 ft.)
8. Mixtur
9. Zimbel

10. Regal (8 ft.)
11. Waldflötgen (1 ft.)
12. Flackflötgen (4 ft.)

Rückpositive (Back Choir)

1. Principal (4 ft.)
2. Mixtur
3. Zimbel
4. Octava (2 ft.)
5. Quinta (9 ft.)
6. Quintadeen (8 ft.)

7. Gedactes (4 ft.)
8. Kleingedactes (2 ft.)
9. Spitzfloite (2 ft.)
10. Siffloite (2 ft.)
11. Trommeten (8 ft.)
12. Singend Regal (4 ft.)

Pedal Organ

1. Principal (16 ft.) bass of Oberwerk (No. 1)
2. Mixtur from Oberwerk
3. Zimbel from Oberwerk
4. Trommeten Bass (8 ft.)

5. Schallmeyen Bass (4 ft.)
6. Zimbel Bass
7. Quintfloite Bass (3 ft.)

The organ of Brescia cathedral, according to Antegnati, only possessed (c. 1580)[1]:

Manual

1. Principal (16 ft.)
2. Principal spezzato (divided between manual and pedals—16–32 ft.)
3. L'Ottava (8 ft.)
4. La Quinta decima (Octava, 4 ft.)
5. La Decima nona (Quinta, 2.2/3 ft.)
6. La Vigesima seconda (Octava, 2 ft.)
7. La Vigesima sesta (Quinta, 1.1/3 ft.)
8. La Vigesima nona (Octava, 1 ft.)

[1] Which agrees with the organ at Milan in 1550 which was registered as: Principal, 8ve, 12th, 14th, 15th, 19th, 22nd, 26th, 29th, 33rd, 36th and Flute 4th. Pedals. Contrabasso 24.

9. Trigesima terza (Quinta, 2/3 ft.)
10. Vigesima seconda (to use with Flauto 8ve, L'Ottava, and La Decima nona, for Cornetto effect)
11. Flauto in quinta decima (4 ft.)
12. Flauto in ottava (8 ft.)

Pedal

1. Principal (16–32 ft.) acting on lower pipes of Manual stop (2).

For full organ, 1, 3, 4, 5, 6, 7, 8, and 9, are recommended; Nos. 3 and 12, for playing in notes of small values (semiquavers, etc.) while Nos. 3 and 12, with an added tremulant stop (not at Brescia), could be used for slower pasages. No. 12 could act as a solo stop, and Nos. 2 and 12 for a 'dialogue' between manual and pedal. These stops were much quieter, though reedier, than our own.

It is worth mentioning the type of stops suggested by Diruta in his 'Il Transilvano' (1609) for the twelve ecclesiastical tones, together with what was supposed to be their characteristic qualities:

Name	*Stops*	*Character*
Tone I. (Dorian) D to D. Final D.	Principal (16 ft.) Ottava (8 ft.), Flauto or Principal.	Full sounding.
Tone II. (Hypodorian) A to A. Final D.	Principal (16 ft.) Tremulant.	Melancholy.
Tone III. (Phrygian) E to E. Final E.	Principal (16 ft.) Flauto (8 ft.).	Mournful.
Tone IV. (Hypophrygian) B to B. Final E.	Principal (16 ft.) Tremulant.	Gloomy and dejected.
Tone V. (Lydian) F to F. Final F.	Ottava (8 ft.) Quinta decima (4 ft.) Flauto.	Moderate gaiety.

PLATE VII

SOME 16TH CENTURY ORGANS

Name	Stops	Character
Tone VI. (Hypolydian) C to C. Final F.	Principal (16 ft.) Ottava (8 ft.) Flauto.	Excites devotion.
Tone VII. (Mixolydian) G to G. Final G.	Ottava (8 ft.) Quinta decima (4 ft.) Vigesima seconda (2 ft.).	Mild and lively.
Tone VIII. (Hypomixolydian) D. to D. Final G.	Flauto, or Flauto and Ottava (8 ft.) or Flauto and Principal (16 ft.), or Flauto and Quinta decima (4 ft.).	Free and agreeable.
Tone IX. (Aeolian) A to A. Final A.	Principal (16 ft.) Quinta decima (4 ft.) Vigesima seconda (2 ft.).	Free and agreeable.
Tone X. (Hypoaeolian) E to E. Final A.	Principal (16 ft.) Ottava (8 ft.) or Flauto.	Sombre.
Tone XI. (Ionian) C to C. Final C.	Flauto, or Flauto and Quinta decima (or with Vigesima seconda), Ottava, Quinta decima and Vigesima seconda.	Agreeable and lively.
Tone XII. (Hypoionian) G to G. Final C.	Flauto, Ottava, Quinta decima, or Flauto (8 ft.) alone.	Agreeable and lively.

See also these important works on organs: Mueren (Van der) *Het orgel in der Nederlanden* (Leuven), 1931, pp. 153–194; Dufourcq (N), *Esquisse d'une histoire de l'orgue en France*, 1935; Klotz (H.), *Über die Orgelkunst der Gotik, der Renaissance, und der Barock*, 1934; also Williams (C. F. Abdy), *The Story of the Organ*, 1903.

An important positive organ of this time was the 'Regal', an instrument with reed pipes as opposed to the ordinary 'flue' pipes of the earlier portative organ. It was more expressive, and capable of a certain degree of diminuendo and crescendo, which presumably added to its popularity.

THE CLAVICEMBALO AND CLAVICHORD (MANICORDO)

Much less is known about the music for the cembalo or harpsichord and kindred instruments than we should like. The pieces in the Hans Kotter collection (*c.* 1513–35), if for clavichord, are possibly the first. The Attaignant collection (1530) is written for 'Orgues, Espinettes, Manicordion', and there is an 'Intabulatura nova . . . per Arpichordi, Clavicimbali, Spinette, e Manachordi', dated 1551. There is also an 'Intavolatura di Cimbalo' (1576) by Antonio Valente; but few works written for clavicembalo are found before 1580. In England and Spain, with the Fitzwilliam collection (*c.* 1550–1621) and My Ladye Nevell's Booke (1591), and Cabezón's 'Obras' (1577), these instruments seem to have been taken more seriously. It is not possible to affirm that the Italian masters, like the Gabrielis or Merulo, ever played the clavicembalo, though it is more than probable that they did, seeing that both Andrea and Giovanni Gabrieli's Ricercari (1595–6) are marked 'for all kinds of keyed instruments'. Moreover they possessed fine instruments, like one in the Victoria and Albert Museum which is of Venetian make (1574), and measures 7 ft. 4 in. (see P. James's *Early Keyboard Instruments*, London, 1930). Diruta mentions that cembalos were mostly used by dance musicians, who used metal plectrums and struck the keys instead of pressing them as organists did. He recommends that 'quills' should be used, which were 'quieter' and 'easy speaking', and that appropriate 'shakes' and 'graces' should be employed.

THE ORGANISTS OF ST. MARK'S, VENICE

The Venetian composers were linked by following one another either as the musical directors of St. Mark's (Maestro di Cappella), or by succeeding to the position of 1st or 2nd organist, as well as being pupils of the same school.

Thus, Willaert was 'maestro di cappella' at St. Mark's until 1562. Cipriano de Rore succeeded him, occupying the post until his death in 1565. He was followed by Zarlino, the famous theorist and author of 'L'Istitutioni Armoniche' (1558) to 1590. Baldassare Donato followed from 1590, Giovanni Croce in 1603, Martinengo in 1609, and Monteverdi, the first great composer of opera, in 1613. Whether an organist was 1st or 2nd is not always ascertainable, the documents being vague on the point. It seems that Claudio Merulo succeeded Parabosco as 2nd organist in 1557 and that he took over the position as 1st organist on Padovano's departure in 1566, Andrea Gabrieli assuming the place of 2nd organist. Merulo left Venice on Nov. 1st, 1584, and it appears that Andrea's nephew, Giovanni Gabrieli, succeeded him two months later. Andrea died in 1586, to be followed by Bell'haver and later Guami.

The following table presents such information as we have:

1st Organist	2nd Organist
Zuane di Maria (1502–1507)	Alvise Arciero (1503–1530)
Dionisio Memo (1507–1516)	
Frate Giovanni Armonio (Crocicchieri) (1516–1552)	
	Giulio Segni (1530–1533)
	Baldassare da Imola (1533–1541)
	Jachet Buus, 1505–1564 (1541–1551)
	Girolamo Parabosco, 1525–c. 1600 (1551–1557)
Annibale Padovano, 1527–1600 (1552–1566)	Claudio Merulo, 1533–1604 (1557–1566)

1st Organist	2nd Organist
Claudio Merulo (1566–1584. 1st Nov.)	Andrea Gabrieli, 1510–1586 (1566–1586)
Giovanni Gabrieli, 1557–1612 (1585 (1st Jan.)–1612)	Vicenzo Bell'haver (1586–1588)
	Gioseffo Guami, 1540–1611 (1588–1591)
	Paulo Giusto (1591–1624)

The Maestri di Cappella in order of succession were:

Pietro de Fossis - - - - -	1491–1527
Adrian Willaert,1480–1562 - - -	1527–1562
Cipriano de Rore, 1516–1565 - -	1562–1565
Zarlino, 1517–1590 - - - -	1565–1590
Baldassare Donato, 1548–1605 - -	1590–1603
Giovanni Croce, 1557–1609 - - -	1603–1609
G. Martinengo (?) - - - - -	1609–1613
Monteverdi, 1567–1643 - - -	1613–1643

Among many names associated with the Venetian school those that principally concern us are Andrea Gabrieli (the Uncle), Claudio Merulo and Giovanni Gabrieli (the nephew).

Cipriano de Rore, a pupil of Willaert's, together with Buus and Andrea Gabrieli, was an important writer of madrigals and motets, but of no known organ works. He comes mid-way between the first and second Venetian schools, and is known for his use of chromaticisms in a series of madrigals based on a twelve-tone system commended by Zarlino.

Annibale Padovano[1] (1527–1600), is a composer in whom interest has recently been revived. His style much resembles that of Merulo, whom he probably influenced, though his compositions are not so strong or developed as the latter's. He was one of the

[1] He is often referred to merely as Annibale.

earliest members of the second Venetian school, and published a set of instrumental ricercari in 1556. His organ 'Toccate e Ricercari', however, did not come out until 1604.

The line of division between the first and second schools may be drawn about 1550–1560, when Padovano and Merulo became organists and Zarlino Maestro di Cappella.

ANDREA GABRIELI

Andrea Gabrieli (1510–1586) was a native of Venice and a member of a famous family of musicians. He became a pupil of Willaert's, like Buus perhaps, de Rore and Parabosco, and was a member of St. Mark's choir in 1536. In 1566 he succeeded Claudio Merulo as 2nd organist, though 23 years his senior. As a composer he was greatly respected, his fame spreading as far as Germany and the Netherlands. In 1574 he was commissioned to compose a cantata and a Magnificat for the reception of Henry III of France at Venice. He remained the most important Venetian composer until his death in 1586.

It is said that he assisted Marenzio, the famous madrigal writer, to compose marriage music for Francesco, son of Cosimo de Medici, in 1579. Francesco came from Florence, in the company of many Florentine notables, but the music was unsatisfactory— they thought it too serious or inexpressive for a wedding. This led to a conversation between Galilei and Zarlino on the evident inadequacy of the madrigal or motet for the full expression of human emotions. The spirit of the age led to those famous meetings at Count Bardi's house where, as all the history books tell us, the foundation of opera was laid, though traces of it can be seen right through the fifteenth and sixteenth centuries. He was also on very friendly terms with Orlandus Lassus.

Andrea Gabrieli's compositions are of rich and glorious quality. Perhaps better than those of any other composer they represent old Venice in all its sumptuousness. Under Willaert's influence he wrote for two or three choirs and was one of the first to exploit the writing for instruments on a large scale. Historically he comes midway between the first and second schools, but aesthetically he belongs to the latter, and although he was older than its other principals he did as much for the advancement of music as any of them. He was a prolific composer, and developed every then known form of composition, for voices, instruments and organ.

As well as the general richness of effect in all Andrea's compositions, we observe a pronounced thematic interest which distinguishes them from the endless stream of counterpoint of the earlier masters. In the 'Canzon Ariosa' in his third book of Ricercari (1596), for instance, there are characteristic themes which he works out with a skill that amounts to nothing less than genius.

Andrea Gabrieli's ricercari are austere, though full of beauty. They follow the style of the older school.

Ex. XLIX (Ricercare on the 4th tone)

In his canzoni and other compositions, however, he is composing music that looks towards another age. Not that all his compositions are supremely valuable. Some, like the Intonations, are merely meant for everyday use (Intonationi d'organo, 1593); and the simple toccatas for educational purposes, as found in Diruta's 'Il Transilvano' (1597), although attractive, are not in his finest vein. Of other works, such as those in his 'Canzoni alla Francese' (1571 and the two 1605 volumes), the 2nd and 3rd books of Ricercari (1595 and 1596) and those in the tablature books of Bernard Schmidt (1607) and J. Woltz, only a few have as yet been restored to light. Some organ pieces, again, still remain in manuscript at the Munich and Berlin State Libraries. His most important works are possibly the 2nd (1595) and 3rd (1596) books of Ricercari, and the 5th and 6th volumes of the 'Canzoni alla Francese' (1605). The 1595 edition contains only ricercari; the next (1596) has 6 ricercari, beside keyboard arrangements of 2 madrigals and a motet, 5 variations on an early passemezzo (rare for Italy), and two interesting works called 'Fantasia Allegra' and 'Canzon Ariosa'. The latter 'Canzoni alla Francese' (1605) contains mostly keyboard settings of madrigals by Lasso, Jannequin and Crequillon, with four compositions called 'Ricercari Ariosi'.

His toccatas have all the characteristics of the Venetian toccata, but are simpler than the later compositions of Claudio Merulo. Yet what could be nobler than this passage from the Toccata on the 6th Tone?

Ex. L (Toccata on the 6th tone)

Such works, containing the essence of Venetian organ music, may be placed beside the best in the literature of the keyboard, however much Merulo and Giovanni Gabrieli were to do in the way of enrichment and development. Many of the elder Gabrieli's toccatas and other works, pre-classical though they may be reckoned, are worthy of being admitted alongside the classics into the modern repertory.

His 'Canzon Ariosa' is a work of genius—a masterpiece almost unique in its time for its interest. As for the exceptional beauty of its themes, here are phrases from the third bar onwards:

Ex. LI (Canzon Ariosa)

And a poignant passage from bars 14 to 18

Ex. LII

illustrates the degree of lyric intensity and expression Gabrieli was capable of attaining within a limited harmony. As much may be said of bars 21 to 23, and the effective imitation of the semiquaver group in bars 26 to 29.

Ex. LIII

What could be finer, simple though it is, than the chords of the thirtieth bar, repeated again at the third bar from the end, with its forecast of tonic and dominant harmony?

Ex. LIV

For the magnificence of its conception and its imitations, it will be hard to find anything more wonderful in the whole era than the passage that follows from bar 32.

PLATE VIII

PRESUMED PORTRAIT OF CLAUDIO MERULO (1533–1604)
by Annibale Carracci (dated 1588)

Ex. LV

A genius, so we say again. An image of Venice in all her glory!

He composed a vast number of masses, madrigals, motets and sacred part-songs, and so on, including a number for voices or instruments or combined instruments. Here is a summary of his known works:

Keyboard

Canzoni alla Francese. Lib. V. 1571 and 1605. Lib. VI, 1605. (Lib. V contains madrigals by Lasso, Jannequin and others, together with ricercari based upon them, and four compositions called 'Ricercari Ariosi'. Lib. VI a 'Madrigale nel fine' and a 'Capriccio a imitatione beliss (ima)', with nine other madrigals.)

Intonationi d'Organo. Lib. I, 1593.

Combined with those of his nephew.

Ricercari di Andrea Gabrieli . . . Lib. II (1585?) 1595 (13 Ricercari 'for all kinds of keyed instruments').

Ricercari di Andrea Gabrieli . . . Lib. III, 1596. (6 Ricercari, including one 'Motteto', 2 'Madrigaletti', and a 'Capriccio

G   B.K.M

sopra il Pass'e mezo Antico, in cinque modi variati', a 'Fantasia
allegra' and a 'Canzon Ariosa'—'for all kinds of keyed instruments'.

Diruta's II Transilvano, 1597 (5 Toccatas).

Bernard Schmidt's Tablature Book (1607) (possibly ornamental).
  2 Toccatas on the 5th and 6th Tones, a 'Fuga Quarta' and others.

J. Woltz: Nova Musices Organicae Tablatura, 1617 (11 pieces).

(Instrumental or those employing instruments)

Sacrae Cantiones . . . tum generis instrumentis cantatu commo-
dissimae . . . (5 voices), 1565–84–90.

Madrigali et Ricercari (4 voices), 1587 (7 ricercari).

Psalmi Davidici . . . tum omnis generis instrumentorum, tunc
ad vocis modulationem, accomodati . . . (1583–1606).

Canti Concerti . . . per voci e strumenti musicali . . . (6–16 voices)
1587 (containing a vocal 'Alla Battaglia' (Battle piece), for 8
voices, and an instrumental 'Ricercar per sonar a 8', with 10
pieces by his nephew).

Also in: Gardano (A) Dialoghi Musicali, 1590 (containing 2 battle
pieces for 8 wind instruments by Andrea Gabrieli and Annibale
Padovano).

MSS. of Keyboard Works

Berlin State Library, MS. 191. Organ Book containing a canzon
and ricercari.

Munich Library, MS. 132. Motet followed by 3 organ pieces.
(For MSS. of Choral Works, see Eitner's Quellen-Lexicon.
Also list of 85 vocal works in Eitner's Bibl.)

CLAUDIO MERULO

Claudio Merulo (1533–1604), one of the most poetic figures of
the age and perhaps the greatest organist of the sixteenth century,
raised organ playing and keyboard technique to a standard of
artistry never previously attained. He was born at Correggio in
1533, and we often see his name printed as 'Claudio da Correggio'.
His family name was Merlotti, but Merulo was the name generally

given to him. He was a pupil of Girolamo Donati and Tutualle Menon, and at the age of 23 became organist at Brescia cathedral. A year later, after a contest with 9 other candidates, he became 2nd organist at St. Mark's, Venice (1557) in collaboration with Padovano, who was then 1st organist.

About this time many improvements were effected. We call the period that of the 2nd Venetian school. The Flemish influence had passed, and Italians took over the reins. Willaert died in 1562, and Cipriano de Rore took his place. In the same year Zarlino became director (1565). In 1566, it seems that Merulo was appointed 1st organist, Andrea Gabrieli being the 2nd. At about this time we begin to find the mention of instruments, or a cembalo, in printed music. So it is possible that these masters did much to influence the change that was then perhaps greatly desired.

An anecdote is told by Zarlino, in his 'l'Istitutioni Armoniche', of how young Merulo was introduced to Willaert to join in a discussion on Zarlino's new theories. On an evening in mid-May Zarlino waited on St. Mark's square to present Merulo, 'the sweetest organist of our time,' to a certain Francesco Viola, a composer and a friend of Willaert's. Viola was to accompany them to the house of the then aged Willaert who, although kept in by gout, was holding a reception and, as they said, was willing to discuss the theories in Zarlino's illustrious book.[1]

During his first year as 1st organist, Merulo seems to have begun activities as a publisher in association with a certain Betanio (1566). They brought out the works of Verdelot and Portia, composers of the old Flemish school, together with some madrigals of his own. He also constructed an organ of his own design with four stops. This, remarkably enough, is still in existence, and was in working order so lately as 1867.

Merulo enjoyed a great reputation as a teacher. Students came from all parts of Italy and from Germany and Northern Europe to hear him and study his methods. It is said that 'he overwhelmed the learned and unlearned alike'. For a generation, keyboard technique was largely based upon the easy, flowing style of

[1] See Grove's Dict. Article on Merulo.

his compositions. The next great advance was made by Fresco-baldi.

Diruta, the author of 'Il Transilvano', said that Merulo trans-formed his conception of organ playing, both from a technical and an artistic point of view. According to Diruta, he played with 'ease and gravity, and fingers bent'. The instructions in the pre-face of his 'Il Transilvano' direct that (*a*) the arm was to be held straight and should guide the hand over the keyboard, (*b*) the fin-gers should be slightly curved, and (*c*) that the hand was to be light and relaxed, merely resting on the keyboard. He adds that the thumb was not to be used except in passing from an accented to an unaccented note. Merulo's fingering for the scale and the different intervals is given in Chapter X of this work.

Merulo composed many madrigals, masses and motets, but is principally famous for his free and distinctly instrumental com-positions for the organ. His art is best exemplified in his two books of toccatas written on the first 10 tones. These works are character-ized by florid passage-work often of a highly poetic nature, and at times by a poignant expressiveness. Merulo's scale-passages are more subtle and complex than those of his contemporaries. Study of his embroidery shows that he must have had a finely developed technique, as we may see in the following example:

Ex. LVI (Toccata on the 5th tone)

For subtlety and technical attainment this was surpassed only by Frescobaldi.

His compositions have an individual quality which, together with his smoothly flowing passage-work, has caused them to be hailed by some as the earliest independent keyboard music. In justice to the past, this cannot quite be allowed, for many preambles and other works by the early German masters are no less individually instrumental. The bulk of the earlier music, however, —the preambles apart—was written on ecclesiastical or other subjects. The Venetian composers frequently wrote on their own themes—Merulo and Gabrieli particularly.

Merulo's music is excellently formed—witness the Toccata on the 5th tone, one of his finest and best-known works. The opening, even for its age, is exceptionally grand.

Ex. LVII

This is followed by a typical poetic flow of semiquavers, which constitutes the main scheme of the toccata.

Ex. LVIII

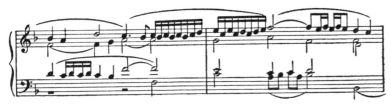

After the final trill of this section a slow middle movement of great lyricism is introduced. (See example LXI, p. 87.) It continues with enriched embellishments and passages reminiscent of the previous section, which develop into fresh and more complicated passage-work in semiquavers. Again the second section is slowly and cleverly resumed. It is slightly more involved, but the same character is maintained.

Ex. LIX

Broader and answering passage-work continues, breaking into a long flow of semiquavers, which work themselves out to the final chord. The scheme is two contrasting subjects, with a development of each section on revival (A':B':A":B": final or A''').

Merulo's toccatas have all the grandeur characteristic of the Venetian toccata, and may be said to represent its highest form. Such passages as these:

Ex. LX*a* (Toccata on the 2nd tone)

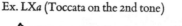

Ex. LX*b* (Toccata on the 5th tone)

with their fine, sweeping phrases, represent a bygone age of beauty. Such a style or school is not less worthy of being played and studied than the works of Scarlatti and Couperin, which are now considered worthy of revival.

Merulo's poetic vein and the subtlety of his passage-work with its various detail, make us think of him as a sixteenth-century Chopin; for Merulo was meticulous in the working-out of his parts. He also shows himself as aware of the system of key-tonality which was dawning upon men's minds. His music is filled with sensitive suspensions. The heights of expressiveness he attained can be illustrated by the lyrical slow section of this same toccata on the 5th tone:

Ex. LXI (Toccata on the 5th tone)

which at the chord marked (*), reaches a poignancy equal to almost anything in the nineteenth century.

Merulo remained 1st organist to St. Mark's until 1585. He then left Venice to become organist to the Duke of Parma, under whose patronage he lived until his death in 1604. There exists a letter giving an account of his death and funeral. On April 25th Merulo was afflicted with a pain in his side. The doctors by deceiving him into the belief that he was being given a syrup, persuaded him to take rhubarb, which only increased the pain. 'How cruelly these doctors have treated me!' he is reported to have said. This was on the 2nd. The pain increased, and he died on May the 4th. He was buried with all solemnity, attended by his pupils who included Alessandro Volpius, Christina Bora, Antonio Bertanelli and Andrea Sulati, the last, however, scarcely 'deigning' to come to the funeral, having only been a pupil for a month. There is a portrait of him by Annibale Carracci in the National Museum at Naples, dated 1588. (See opposite p. 80.) Quiro Bigi reproduces an engraving of Merulo in his work on that artist. (See Bibliography.) Beyond the two books of toccatas (1598–1604) and some early works, few of his compositions have so far been brought back to light.

His organ works consist of:

> Messe d'Intavolatura. Lib. IV, 1568[1].
>
> Ricercari d'Intavolatura d'Organo. Lib. I, 1567. 1605. Lib. II, 1607. Lib. III, 1608.

[1] See Eitner (Quellen-Lexicon)—'*Toccata e Ricercara per Organo*. Libro IV (1568), from the MSS. in the Bibl. de L'ancien Couvent des Augustines de Toulouse. Modern transcription by J. B. Labat (S. Richault) Paris. (See p. 149 in Bibliography of present work.)

Canzoni d'Intavolatura d'Organo. Lib. I, 1592; Lib. II, 1606; and Lib. III, 1611.

Toccate d'Intavolatura d'Organo. Lib. I, 1598; Lib. II, 1604.

Also in:

Schmidt's (Bernard) Tablature Book (1607); Woltz's Tablature Book (1617); and Diruta's 'Il Transilvano' (1625).

MSS. of Organ Works

Berlin State Library.
  W. 36, Nr. 488–97 (10 Toccatas).
Munich State Library.
  Organ arrangement of a motet.
Municipal Library at Thorn.
  In Organ Tablature Book (c. 1594–1605).
  (See Eitner's Quellen-Lexicon for MSS. of vocal music.)

GIOVANNI GABRIELI

In many respects Giovanni Gabrieli (1557–1612) was one of the most refreshing composers of the sixteenth century. Little is known of his life, and the high spirit and golden quality of his music have been somewhat eclipsed by the ecclesiastically canonized Palestrina and his school. Otherwise musicians would realize that for modernity of form, freshness of spirit, sensitiveness and brilliance of setting, Gabrieli's music, together with that of his uncle Andrea and Claudio Merulo, represents some of the finest achievements of the century.

Giovanni was born in 1557. He spent the greater part of his life at Venice, except in 1575–9 when he served at the court of Munich, where he came under the influence of Orlandus Lassus. Known as a musician of merit at 18, he was thought fit at 27 to take Merulo's place as 1st organist (1585), which he apparently retained until his death in 1612.

German composers seem to have been much influenced by him —Hans Leo Hassler (1564–1612), Heinrich Schütz (1585–1672), Michael and Hieronymus Praetorius (1560–1629), Georg Aichinger (1564–1628) and many other German composers who came to study under him. Many of his patrons, too, were Germans— Duke Albert V, William V of Bavaria, and the rich Count Fugger of Augsburg, to whom he dedicated his Sacred Symphonies, 'for having', as he said in his preface, 'invited him to his wedding.' Schütz, Hieronymus Praetorius and Aichinger were his own pupils. Hassler studied with his uncle Andrea. But all imbibed something of his style and spirit—Schütz from the technique and style of his instrumental works and Hassler in the general arrangement of his organ and other compositions. Both these were to do much to build the church music of the German school. Hence it may be said that a large part of Europe took its lead from the Gabrielis; the principal exceptions being Frescobaldi and the then slowly developing Florentine opera.

That Schütz was his most esteemed pupil (from 1609 to 1612), is suggested by the fact that Gabrieli, on his death-bed, bequeathed his signet-ring to him, thus symbolizing, as it has been said, the transference of the classical tradition to the schools of Germany. Schütz's own description of him is as interesting as it is peculiar. 'I served my first year of apprenticeship under the great Gabrieli. Ye immortal Gods! What a man was that! If the ancients, so rich in expression, had been acquainted with his person they would have placed him above Amphion; and if the Muses had so inclined to enter the marriage state Melpomene would have desired no other husband than he, so great was he in his art.' Michael Praetorius called him 'the most eminent and most famous of all musicians'—of his time. (Syntagma Musicum, 1619.)

Gabrieli's compositions can be divided into three groups; vocal, keyboard and general instrumental. The vocal music is not exactly our concern; like his instrumental works, it is the perfect expression of the beauty and pomp of Venice. As to his keyboard music, although no edition was actually printed with his name, there are a number of his compositions among the works of others, as well as those in manuscript. Of these, very few have been transcribed, and like his uncle Andrea's compositions, not all have equal value. Thus the twelve intonations from his uncle's

'Intonationi d'Organo' (1593), in spite of their attractive setting and charm, are the commonplace of Venetian writing. They were, after all, intended only as practical interludes during divine service, and the same may be said of the Toccata on the 2nd tone in Diruta's 'Il Transilvano'—a book of instruction in which highly complicated examples would have been out of place. There is some attractive passage-work in it, which has something of Gabrieli's character, but it is still developed on quite a simple though pleasant Venetian model. On the other hand, the canzon on the theme of the 'La Spiritata' ('Canzone detta la Spiritata'.) which, according to Tagliapietra, was taken from the 1625 edition of Diruta's work,[1] is a work most remarkable for beauty, form and construction. In a manuscript book at Lubbenau [2] which is supposed to contain works by Gabrieli, some, although full of Gabrielian charm, do not rise above the ordinary Venetian level, while others, like the 'Fuga on the 9th tone', and the even more remarkable 'Fantasia on the 6th tone', are so advanced that it is hard to believe they can have been written in Gabrieli's time. This might apply to his famous 'Ricercar on the 10th tone', were it not printed under his name in his uncle's ricercari (Lib. II, 1595). And the same with the instrumental works; for whereas many of the instrumental canzoni, even the famous 'Sonata pian e forte', found in the 1597 edition of his Sacred Symphonies, are grand, pompous and magnificent, they do not compare with the brilliance of certain works in his 'Canzoni et Sonate' and the later Sacred Symphonies, published three years after his death in 1615 (e.g. 'Canzon a 6' and 'Surrexit Christus').

Gabrieli's compositions are characterized by freshness, melodiousness and brilliance. They are the quintessence of the Venetian spirit. Forms that had been cultivated by his predecessors in him reached perfection. Posterity owed much to him, and his melodic sequences and monothematic treatment suggest future developments. Gabrieli had a strong inkling of modern tonality and

[1] See Tagliapietra's *Anthology of Ancient and Modern Pianoforte Music*. Vol. 11. Preface, p. 5. 1931. Also in a tablature in the Vienna State Library. See p. 97.
[2] See p. 92, footnote 1.

harmony, and a sense of modulation. This passage from one of his toccatas

Ex. LXII (Toccata. Lynar Lubbenau. MS 331)

might almost be thought of as a modulation to a new key in the modern sense of the term, and in the instrumental 'Canzon a 6' he reaches out to the harmonic systems of another age:

Ex. LXIII

His sense of sequence was amazing. Starting from an idiom prevalent in his school, he carried it at moments to such inordinate lengths that one feels that he must have looked upon it as a new toy. We find this in the 'Ricercar on the 10th tone', and in

Ex. LXIV (Fantasia on the 6th tone)

passages like the example from a manuscript fantasia (if it be really his),[1] though it is always used with the most pleasing clarity. (See Ex. LXIV.)

A feature of Gabrieli's composition is the employment of a principal theme or melody often of outstanding brilliance. The use by later Venetians of a principal, highly characterized subject has had its sequel throughout the course of the main stream of European music. Here is a fugue-subject worthy of being put alongside many a seventeenth and eighteenth century composition:

Ex. LXV

Obvious though it is, the fact is not borne in mind in all circles that the value of a fugue does not lie only in the working-out of the subject. The beauty of Bach's subjects is not less important than his fugal developments. Gabrieli's appreciation of this is one the qualities which give him (and other Venetians) rank as a founder of classical form. Here is an example from one of Giovanni's major instrumental works:

Ex. LXVI (Surrexit Christus)

Gabrieli's sense of form is best exemplified in his keyboard and instrumental music. In the keyboard toccata he was not always so successful, since he kept more or less within conventional lines. But in the canzon and ricercar he showed more purpose and individuality. The 'Ricercar on the 10th tone', for instance, is a marvel of construction and development. It starts with a fine Gabrielian subject:

[1] This piece is taken from a nineteenth-century MS. in the possession of the Society of the History of Music of the Netherlands, which is said to contain works by Gabrieli copied from the Lynar Library at Lubbenau (Mus. MS. 331).

Ex. LXVII

which is worked into a simple yet impressive counterpoint, and is followed by a series of frequent but pleasant repetitions on the phrase:

Ex. LXVIII

answered in different modes and voices, accompanied by a flow of sequential harmony as fresh and modern as anything in the sixteenth century. Imitations are frequently used in all parts, and in combination with the first subject. This oft-repeated phrase, like the one in the 'Fantasia on the 6th tone', forms the basis of the composition, the first theme being used as a subsidiary background. The coda—a feature of which the Venetians have left us excellent examples—acts as a grand and impressive peroration. This piece and the 'Ricercar on the 8th tone' are the best known of Gabrieli's works. Both come from Andrea Gabrieli's second book of ricercari (1595).

The works in Diruta's 'Il Transilvano' (1597 & 1609) have been mentioned already. The only other keyboard pieces are either in German tablatures (Bernard Schmidt, Junior, 1607, and Jacob Woltz, 1617), or still in manuscript. The Schmidt works are given in highly ornamental form, as the fashion was with German organists, but those in Woltz are without coloratura—'in order to show the composer more effectively', so the work states.

The various manuscripts in different parts of Europe call for caution before we agree in attributing them to Gabrieli. Those from the Dutch source already mentioned, if really by Gabrieli, are remarkable. The 'Fantasia on the 6th tone', for instance, might have been written in the later part of the seventeenth century. It is composed mostly of imitations and echo effects, with a pronounced appreciation of contrast between loud and soft which was becoming so noticeable in Gabrieli and other Italians (e.g. 'Sacred Symphonies'). The rhythm is highly spirited, and its form is clear and divided into sections. The fugue from the same source is another example of Gabrieli's pleasing and refreshing counterpoint. Its two themes mingle with a gracious ease, showing how well Gabrieli understood the working of a subject and countersubject. Of the remaining manuscripts at Berlin, Vienna and Munich, mentioned in Eitner's Quellen-Lexicon, not much can be said. Many of them appear to be copies of others already in print. The British Museum has a manuscript (Add. 29486) which contains, with slight alterations, all the Giovanni intonations from his uncle's Intonationi d'Organo (1593). They are in a French hand, and were completed by September, 1618.

Gabrieli's fame rests, among other things, upon his having been the first composer to introduce an orchestration into a written score, as well as composing music for three or even four choirs. Before him Willaert and others had chiefly written for double choirs. Instruments had been employed in choral music from time immemorial. The term 'concerto' was used for this practice, and the word implied a contrast even in sixteenth-century Italy. But orchestration in the strict sense—that is the precise allotting of parts to different instruments—does not seem to have occurred before Giovanni Gabrieli. The 'Ricercar per sonar' in his uncle Andrea's 'Canti Concerti' (1587) and the pieces in 4 or 5 parts by Maschera and Vicentino are merely textless, like those of many of their contemporaries. But the two issues of the Sacrae Symphoniae published in 1597 and 1615, and the 'Canzoni et Sonate' (1615) contain many pieces scored with instruments named for each part.

The Sacred Symphonies are among the monuments of musical history. In the 1597 set there are 45 vocal and 16 instrumental pieces, 3 of which are fully orchestrated. The 6th instrumental piece is the oft-quoted 'Sonata pian e forte'. Like its companions, it is divided into two parts. The first has 3 trombones and a cornetto, and the other 3 trombones and a violino. This piece is distinguished by the first known direction of 'loud' and 'soft' in a score. The effect was in those days considered as a sort of echo. The 11th and 12th canzoni (Canzon a echo) both have identical groups of 4 cornetti and 1 trombone. These canzoni are really the same piece, with a more elaborate second organ basso in the 12th canzon ('Organo di concerti'), which often does independent work as well as combining with a solo cornetto. The final canzon (No. 16), written for 15 voices, has 3 groups of instruments: (*a*) 4 trombones and 1 cornetto, (*b*) 4 trombones and a violino (an alto sort), and (*c*) 4 trombones and 1 cornetto. The second and last group of Gabrieli's Sacred Symphonies (1615) contains works up to 19 voices. Only five or six instrumental pieces are traceable in the available manuscripts in this country. Winterfeld (1834) published two items of remarkable brilliance from this work; an 'In ecclesis' with 3 cornetti, 2 trombones, a violino part and 2 choruses, and a 'Surrexit Christus', with 4 trombones, 2 cornetti, 2 violino parts and 3 voice parts.

The 'Canzoni et Sonate' (1615) appears to be a later work. It contains 16 instrumental canzoni and 5 sonatas, as well as a sonata 'con tre violini' at the end of the collection. These are even more remarkable than the Sacred Symphonies. The 'Canzon a 6', for instance, is an amazingly brilliant composition. The six instrumental voices are here transcribed in short score.

Ex. LXIX

This canzon is monothematic, with the interspersion of the above quoted chordal passage. The single subject is treated with excellent effect and modulates with brilliance, while the chordal section is grandly impressive. The piece shows what a feeling Gabrieli had for orchestral effects. Monteverdi became director of St. Mark's in 1613, a year after Gabrieli's death. Hardly to be over-estimated is the influence the example of the two Gabrielis might have had upon the great Florentine.

Symphonia or Sinfonia is in the sixteenth-century sense a composition in which there are 'interludes' of instruments. The 'sinfonia' section usually acts as a prelude or postlude to the predominantly vocal portions of a composition. Such are the symphonies of the Monteverdian and other operas. The term 'sonata' had little in common with the modern usage. It indicated a composition to be played as distinguished both from a vocal work (i.e. cantata) and an instrumental form derived from one originally sung (i.e. canzon). Unlike the canzon, it was not written in sections—it was a one-movement instrumental form, thus emphasizing even then its unified nature.

Gabrieli's orchestral compositions are grand, pompous and golden in texture, like the city in which they were created. They evoke the magnificence of the Venetian background. However far from being orchestral in our present-day sense, they have a true instrumental source of inspiration combined with a Gabrielian character, and are probably among the greatest instrumental compositions of the time. The Sacred Symphonies of 1597 may well be considered the first great instrumental works, while the latter collection (1615) and the 'Canzoni et Sonate' (1615) are probably the crown of his life's work. They are among the finest things of all music, and it is sad that they should still need complete publication, apart from appreciation and performance.

Gabrieli's genius has never been properly appreciated by the modern world, outside a few historians. To the average musician he is but a name, and his work, with the exception of a few choral pieces, is practically unknown. Frescobaldi, on the other hand, as we shall see later, is fairly well represented in numerous editions, though his nature is mystical and erudite, while Gabrieli's style is fresh and pleasing, thus lending itself more readily to an immediate response. If Merulo is silver, Gabrieli is golden. Little is known of his life and character, but he must have had a spirit akin to a Botticelli's in its freshness. History has yet to tell us more about this glorious age.

PLATE IX

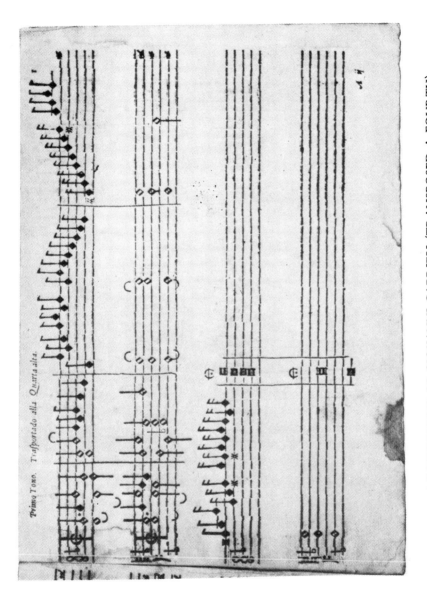

FIRST INTONATION OF GIOVANNI GABRIELI (TRANSPOSED A FOURTH)

From Intonationi d'organo di Andrea Gabrieli, (1593)

His compositions, many of which were published with those of his uncle, are:

Organ and Keyboard

Intonationi d'Organo di Andrea Gabrieli. Lib. I, 1593. (12 Intonations of Giovanni's.)

Ricercari di Andrea Gabrieli . . . Lib. II, 1595 (for all kinds of keyed instruments) (2 ricercari by Giovanni on the 8th and 10th tones).

Diruta's Il Transilvano, 1597–1609–25.

Schmidt (Bernard, Jr.) Tablature Book, 1607 (for organ and keyed instruments) (probably ornamented).

Woltz (J.) Nova Musices Organicae Tabulatura, 1617 (not coloured or ornamented).

Instrumental

Canzoni per sonar a quattro, 1580. (See Einstein (A.) Antiqua. Eine Sammlung alter Musik, 1933.)

Sacrae Symphoniae . . . tam vocibus quam instrumentis (6–16 voices) (new edition) 1597. (14 instrumental canzoni (8–16 voices) with 2 sonatas (8–15 voices)).

Symphoniae Sacrae (6–19 voices), 1615.

(Containing pieces for voices and instruments combined, in at least an In Ecclesis, Christus Surrexit, Jubilate Deo, Quem Vidistis, and a Suscipe.)

Canzoni et Sonate (3–22 voices), 1615. (All parts in Kassel Library, 13 at Berlin and Augsburg.) (16 instrumental canzoni and 5 sonatas with one Sonata a tre violini' with *ad lib* bass.)

MSS. (Keyboard and Instrumental)

Berlin State Library.

MS. 191. Organ Compositions. (See Andrea Gabrieli.)

MS. Catalogue of Winterfeld: 'Partitur aus Concerti.' Bd. 26–8, 33 and 59 (Bd. 26 has a 'Scherza Amarilli e Clori' (?)) (presumably instrumental).

Vienna State Library. Cod. 10110 fol. 34–5.

Toccata. La Inspiritata (MS. in Tablature of Rudolph Lasso).

H   B.K.M.

Library of Institute of Church Music, Breslau.

Bd. 81. Vol. 2. Canzoni et Sonata (?) (Eitner's Quellen–Lexicon).
Munich State Library.

MS. 262. 6 Fugues (?) and 1 Ricercar.

MS. 264. 3 Motets in tablature.

Kassel State Library.

Fol. No. 51 (*b*). Surrexit Christus (presumably instrumental).

Fol. No. 59 (*h*). Ricercar.

Fol. No. 60 (*e*). Sonata a 15 voci.

Fol. No. 147 (*a*). Canzon a 8, Canzon a 12 (presumably instrumental with other MSS. in same library). (From previously
mentioned works.) (Quellen-Lexicon.)

British Museum, London.

ADD. 29486.

Intonations, copied by a French hand from the Giovanni items
in his uncle's 'Intonationi d'Organo', (1593), with 2 fantasias
by Sweelinck.

Lynar Library, Lubbenau.

MS. No. 331.

Also 11 compositions by G. Gabrieli, with 6 songs in 4 voices by
Hans Heugel, copied by Moritz Hauptmann at the Brussels
Conservatory. MS. No. XY. 15030. As well as an organ fantasia
on the 4th tone by Gabrieli with those of Sweelinck and Phil-
lips (MS. U. 11303).

(For complete list of vocal and choral MSS. see Eitner's Quellen-
Lexicon and the 80 vocal works given in Eitner's Bibliography.
Also author's article on 'Gabrieli' in the *Music Review*, May,
1947, p. 100.)

Contemporary Keyboard Composers

Many other excellent composers of keyboard music were associated, or at any rate, contemporary with the Venetian schools, such
as Jachet de Berchem, famous organist to the Duke of Ferrara,
(*fl.* 1545–60), Gioseffo Guami (*c.* 1540–1611), 2nd organist in G.
Gabrieli's time, who was declared by Zarlino to be 'the sweetest of

all players'; Maschera, organist at Brescia, Luzzaschi (1557–1607), the famous master of Frescobaldi, many of whose toccatas are very fine works, and Quagliati, the Roman harpsichordist. Diruta (1560–1637) the author of 'Il Transilvano' (1597) belongs to this period, and the famous Antegnati (1557–1625). In England, William Byrd (1543–1623), although very far away from the Venetian school, is truly worthy of being compared with the great masters of Italy, while his school was equal to any in Europe outside Italy. Of this school we shall speak later.

PART III

THE NORTH EUROPEAN SCHOOLS
AND
THE BEGINNINGS OF THE BAROQUE

CHAPTER VII

SONG AND DANCE FORMS—THE VARIATION FORM

The secular and monodic tendency of music which became so pronounced in the sixteenth century had its origins far back in the past. While dances like the Pavana and Saltarello can be traced back to Spinacino's lute tablature of 1507, and to the Kotter manuscripts for keyboard usage, they must, long before that, have been played as instrumental pieces. The saltarello as an instrumental dance was cultivated by the fourteenth-century Florentines (see p. 16), and dances like the Basse-Danse, Branle, Ballo and Piva, the music of which comes down to us from the early sixteenth century, had been danced throughout the fifteenth century.[1] The sixteenth was the century of lute music, which included much dance music and which spread and multiplied in all parts of Europe. From Luis Milan in Spain, Hans Gerle in Germany and Attaignant in France, lute music grew as pianoforte music did in the nineteenth century. The lute was by far the most popular domestic instrument of the day, and it devolves upon the history of sixteenth-century keyboard music to trace the influence of lute technique on the practice of clavichord and virginal. The early pieces for domestic keyboards have a great similarity to the lute style. The custom of arranging dance music for consorts of viols spread to serious keyboard music. Collections like the English and German keyboard works and certain smaller Italian tablatures illustrate the point. Ammerbach's tablature (1571) contains galliards and passemezzi, as well as serious organ music. By about 1580 the dance forms were well established in keyboard music.

The dance music like the lute music of the period was written mainly for the popular taste and was not all of the best quality. It is a mistake, then, to quote small dance pieces as representative of

[1] See Curt Sachs' *World History of the Dance*. Also Closson (E) *Le Manuscrit dit des Basses Danses de la Bibliothèque de Bourgogne*, 1912, and Blaume (F.), *Studien—Orchestersuite im 15 und 16 Jahr*, 1925.

the best of the early keyboard music. While the polyphonic works of the church musicians are the highest achievements of the age, the ricercari, canzoni and toccatas represent the finest keyboard music. There are some charming dance pieces in the Attaignant collections. In Italy we find attractive ones in an 'Intabulatura nova di varie sorti di balli da sonare per Arpichordi' . . . (1551); but not much as yet has been brought to light until we come to Frescobaldi's brilliant harpsichord dances. In Germany some delightful forms are to be found in the works of Ammerbach (1571) and Normiger (1598), while in England the Elizabethans and Jacobeans produced some very remarkable examples. Pieces by Byrd, Farnaby and Bull contain melodies of outstanding beauty. They come, however, at the end of the Renaissance.

Folk-tunes and other melodies, either in simple statement or in variation form, began to come into keyboard music at the end of the century. Something of the sort occurred in early sixteenth-century works, but the self-subsistent melody is peculiarly characteristic of the Northern European and English schools at which we have now arrived, both of which may have been influenced by innovating tendencies as in Spain. The serious Italian keyboard composers did not use 'tunes' as such, or cultivate the variation form. The 'Pass' e mezo Antico, in cinque modi variati' . . . from the 3rd book of Ricercari of Andrea Gabrieli (1596) is an exception. The four-part instrumental Passemezzi of Bendusi (1553) and Phalese (1571 and 1583), however, were always in four or five 'modi' or 'variants'. Certain German dances possessed variants as a sort of after-dance, and occasional variations are found in some of the Italian lute composers in the middle of the century. The Spanish composers, however, not only used popular tunes freely, but also had a tendency towards harmonic and other variations. The variations in Spain are first found in the lute works of Narvaez (1538) and Mudarra (1546) and later in the collected keyboard and other pieces of Antonio Cabezón (1577). These were called 'diferencias' —differences, being variations in the rhythmic as well as harmonic texture. A type of variation is discernable in Silvestro Ganassi's works for flute (1535); and Diego Ortiz (Spanish again) gave

PLATE X

ILLUMINATED PAGE OF THE ARTS AND SCIENCES WITH
ILLUSTRATION OF A POSITIVE ORGAN
From a German book on the Philosopher's Stone (1582)

rules for the 'division on a ground' in his work 'Tratado de Glosas' (1553). These, however, are mostly a division of an upper part into a small number of notes, as in the different species of counterpoint. They no doubt contributed to the development of the proper variation on a theme. A particular type of organ appeared in Spanish music, called 'Partidos', in which two halves of a manual, each having a different set of stops, were employed. One half, which had all the brilliant stops, was called the 'glosarda', since it dealt with the passage-work (Glosa = variant or running passage), the other only accompanying on some simple flue stops. Arab musicians, who influenced the Spaniards right down to the fifteenth century, called what we term the 'ornamentation' of a theme the 'glos'. We shall see that Frescobaldi used the term 'partitas' (partire = to divide), for his keyboard variations.

Hence it is no surprise to find, next door to the Spanish Netherlands, Pieterszoon Sweelinck composing variations on Dutch airs. How the variation first came to attract English musicians can only be guessed. From Spain? From the Netherlands? From Cabezón, whose patron was Philip, Mary Tudor's husband? We do not know; but it would have been strange if our Elizabethans, who were alive to all European currents, had missed it.

Not much is known of Spanish influence on Italian musicians. Ramos de Pareja (c. 1440–1521), who proposed the theory of equal temperament,[1] was well known to the Italian theorists. He taught in Rome and Bologna, and Spataro was his pupil. The Spanish Kingdom of Naples patronized the famous Gaforus and Tinctoris. Hotby (c. 1487), the English theorist, was both in Spain and Italy. Many Spanish musicians and singers practised at Rome, Naples and elsewhere in Italy, throughout the sixteenth and seventeenth centuries. In Frescobaldi's day the choirmaster of St. Peter's, Rome (1630–48), and the master of the papal chapel (c. 1625), were both Spaniards. Musicians like G. M. Trabaci (fl. 1600), a native of Naples and an experimenter in chromaticism, may be mentioned

[1] It is suggested that Ramos de Pareja got his idea of equal temperament from the division of the Spanish lute frets into semitones. Bermudo refers to this in his theoretical works.

in this connection, and A. Mayone (*fl.* 1600), another Neapolitan. Both composed in a manner very similar to the Spanish tablatures, and at the same time not unlike Frescobaldi's methods. They were, so Willi Apel thinks, a link between the schools of Spain and Rome (see *Musical Quarterly*, Oct., 1938).

Chapter VIII

THE NORTH EUROPEAN SCHOOLS. THE NETHER-LANDS AND ENGLAND.

Jan Pieterszoon Sweelinck

Jan Pieterszoon Sweelinck (1562–1621), succeeded his father as organist at Amsterdam c. 1580, a few years before Giovanni Gabrieli's appointment at St. Mark's. Sweelinck was the Venetian's junior by only five years, but his music belongs to a later age.[1] He had a great admiration for Giovanni's music, but he may also have derived from local sources—such as the lesser known German and Netherlandish composers—Danckerts, perhaps, or Hubert Waelrant (1517–1595)—or possibly from Spain or even England. His work has little direct similarity to the Venetian school.

Sweelinck's music was for long forgotten, like that of so many of the older masters, but through the efforts of the Society for the History of the Music of the Netherlands all his works were eventually published by Breitkopf & Härtel in 12 volumes, the first of which was devoted to his organ or clavier works.[2]

His keyboard pieces include ricercari, fantasias, toccatas and capriccios, including some on chromatic subjects which became popular about this time, as well as variations on Netherlandish songs for the clavicembalo. Four of his compositions were published in the Fitzwilliam Virginal Book.

He spent his life at Amsterdam, where he was greatly admired and referred to as the 'Glory of Amsterdam'. The authorities increased his income in 1586 and again in 1590, and in 1604 the merchants of the city made up a purse for him. Later they presented him with a clavicembalo, together with a finely woven

---

[1] At 15 he became a pupil of Zarlino for theory, and Andrea Gabrieli for organ playing. Hassler says that the Venetian musicians took an interest in him at an early age.

[2] A few also are published in Vol. IX. There has been a recent reissue of his works by G. Alsbach & Co., Amsterdam, 1943.

cloth to cover it. It is recorded that 'everyone was proud to have
known, seen and heard the man'. His character was loveable, and the
fineness of his playing affected everyone fortunate enough to
hear him. John Bull probably submitted to his influence and a
warm friendship sprang up between them. As much may be said
of the English organist, Peter Philips. Samuel Scheidt and Scheidemann were his pupils, and he is generally recognized as the
founder of the North German school of organists. His treatise on
composition has been reprinted in the 10th volume of the Breitkopf & Härtel edition. He died in 1621. In Sweelinck's work we
are in the seventeenth century. The older polyphony had had its
day, and we have our first taste of that austere sublime style which
later developments make us think of as characteristically German.
Sweelinck's music is indeed very Bachian in feeling, with its intense Northern style. His texture is more modern than that of the
previously mentioned Italians and, like Frescobaldi, he was a great
harmonic innovator, and delighted in chromaticism, as we see in
his amazing 'Fantasia Cromatica'.

Chromatic harmony had been experimented with in the chromatic madrigals of de Rore, Marenzio, Vicentino and others, on
the basis of the new harmonic theories of Vincentio and Zarlino;
and hence, too, the chromatic styles of Monteverdi and Gesualdo a
generation later. Chromatic themes and harmonies had a vogue
in the keyboard music of the early part of the seventeenth century, and it is possible that this was derived from the examples
of those earlier Venetians. The chief keyboard musicians to em-
ploy chromatic themes were Sweelinck, Frescobaldi and certain
English musicians. The sources may have been Italian, but it is
more than possible that they were Spanish, for passages like the
following

Ex. LXX

are found in Cabezón but are unusual in the Italian keyboard music of the time. A resemblance, if a faint one, is seen to Sweelinck's chromatic harmony as found in the above fantasia, e.g.

Ex. LXXI (Fantasia Cromatica)

(After Seiffert)

In the length of his compositions and technical style Cabezón's son Hernando still more resembles Sweelinck.

Sweelinck's 'Fantasia Cromatica' is a massive work. For many years it was the earliest music found in the repertory of modern organists. It is long, as Sweelinck's keyboard pieces usually are, and it demands careful execution if a faithful interpretation is to be attained. Sweelinck has been accused of waywardness, and it is true that his grand poetic ruggedness carries us along a more adventurous and imaginative path than the assured and easy-going serenity of the Italians. In some ways he is more attractive than Frescobaldi, by reason of his warmth of character and the fine sweep of his passage-work, which is both austere and poetic. Frescobaldi's music is more inspired, yet contemplative.

Sweelinck's 'Toccata on the 1st tone' is perhaps a still better example of his normal style. The opening is austere and dignified. It is followed by an impressive trill, forming the bridge to an exceptionally fine sequence of motives which is of a grandeur almost worthy of Bach himself. Such a movement, extremely simple though it is, makes one realise that the Dutch master is still inadequately appreciated.

Ex. LXXII (Toccata on the 1st tone)

This is followed by toccata-like passage-work of a more modern kind, and great care must be taken by the executant over the phrasing of each part to achieve a proper interpretation. The next section is written in the typical half-note values of the slow fugal movement of a toccata. It is based on a quasi-chordal formation in four parts, while the Italians generally wrote their second sections in free moving counterpoint. This dignified, closely knit harmony produces a grand effect, and is as characteristic of Sweelinck as any of his passage-work.

Ex. LXXIII

After the fugal section the semiquaver movement is resumed, but is this time of a different pattern. The mode of each passage is generally maintained, and as a whole the modulation is more defined than in the earlier type of toccata. At bar 84 there is a fine sweeping passage for the left hand which, although simple, has a dramatic feeling about it.

Ex. LXXIV

A series of slowly climbing semiquavers leads to the final chord on D.

Sweelinck's figuration at once suggests his great executive gifts, which, with his love of striking effects, gave him a position as a virtuoso that was probably rivalled only by Frescobaldi's, and it is easy to understand how by his massiveness, his brilliance and his poetic waywardness he enthralled the audiences of his time. The power of expression, too, which his music reveals, must have been an outstanding quality of this fascinating and much neglected genius of Amsterdam. He was in the full spirit of the North with its clarity of mind and thoroughness of detail, yet he represented all the warmth of a Dutch interior, and was in his way a worthy progenitor of that which was to follow.

The only compositions printed in his lifetime seem to have been:

Chansons Françaises (3 voices) 1584–92–94.
Pseaumes de David . . . (4–8 parts) Livres I–IV, 1604–13–14–21–23.
Psalms (4 and 6 voices) 1618. 1616.
Rimes Françoises et Italiennes . . . (2–3 parts), . . . avec une Chanson (4 parts). 1612.
Cantiones Sacrae (5 voices), 1619.
Chansons (5 parts) (Copenhagen) and Chansons Vulgaires, Livre VIII, 1608.

And songs for various occasions such as:

Marriage Songs in honour of J. Praetorius and Margaret a Campis (1608); and Joh Stoboeus and David Moller (1616).

Also in:

Phalese's Ghirlanda, 1601. (See Eitner's Quellen-Lexicon for later works, and Tiedeman.)

––––––––

The most important contemporaries around Sweelinck were Hans Leo Hassler (1564–1612), G. M. Trabaci (fl. 1603–1615), John Bull (1563–1628), and Adriano Banchieri (1565–1634).

Hassler, considered as the forefather of the German school, wrote under the direct influence of Venice some ricercari and canzoni for organ. These, though excellent, are not outstanding. He is strong, effective and distinct in key, but his talent went mainly into the choral works upon which his fame rests. Of greater importance, perhaps, were the interesting instrumental balletti, galliards and intrades which he published in his 'Lustgarten neuer teutscher Gesang' in 1601.

Trabaci wrote some excellent music in an advanced style including some chromatic works (Tablatura, Book I, 1603. Book II, 1615); while in Banchieri we recognize a modern outlook and progressiveness in form and phrasing. His works, often quite light, have in them the beginnings of another age.

Mention must also be made of the Frenchman Titelouze (1563–1638), Christian Erbach (1570–1635), an excellent composer of organ music in the Veneto-German style, and the Englishman John Bull (1563–1628) whose brilliant and individual compositions for the organ and virginal place him in the front rank in the instrumental history of our country. Orlando Gibbons (1583–1625), rather later in date, was a composer of finer quality, if not of such virtuosic gifts. It would be better, though, to treat him as belonging to the Frescobaldi period.

THE ENGLISH SCHOOL

The English keyboard schools maintained an individual character, not coming directly under the influence of the Italian Renaissance until quite late in the century. The rays that spread from Italy were, as in the other countries of Europe, used to enrich the English art-forms rather than as direct models. The English developments were generally about 20 or 30 years behind the Italian, but when that influence did come the exemplar was frequently surpassed.

Such Continental influences as directly affected our later Tudor composers for the keyboard probably came from Northern Europe, France and the Spanish-dominated Netherlands, if not from Spain itself. English keyboard forms had little likeness to Italian types, apparent similarities in figuration being common to all Europe, whereas the passage-work of John Bull and Peter

PLATE XI

MVSICA MORTALES RECREAT DIVOSQ BEATOS

a

b

LATE 16TH CENTURY GROUPS

a. Four singers with virginal and lute

b. Virginal with lute, transverse flute and singer

Philips shows definite similarities to that of Sweelinck. Even if the Coranto and other forms were originally Italian, they probably reached us by way of Northern Europe. Reference has already been made to the contacts with Spain consequent upon Mary Tudor's marriage with Philip II.[1] While it would be extravagant to make too much of this, it is noteworthy that the variation form, employed so profusely by the English virginalists, was almost completely absent on the Continent except for Spain, the Dutch Sweelinck and a few keyboard composers of the Spanish court at Naples. These Neapolitans, it may be mentioned, had a predilection for the cembalo rather than the organ and, as in Frescobaldi's later works, their title pages were often marked 'cembalo or organ', instead of the earlier use of 'organ or cembalo'. It is also noteworthy that the English preference was for the plucked type of instruments. The French, with their constant contacts with England and their various publications of 'espinette' music by Attaignant (1530), may also have influenced the English virginalists. The instrumental pieces in the earlier English manuscripts often have French titles, and the French dances have more similarity to the Elizabethan type than to that of Italy and other Southern countries.

If, on the other hand, the virginal compositions of the Royal Appendix 58 (Brit. Mus.) give a clue to the type of music used in England in the first half of the sixteenth century, it is possible that an independent style of keyboard music was maintained throughout English history. The date of the manuscript, however, is vague—for Hughe Aston, the composer of the 'Hornpype' variations given in this work, may not be the priest who died in 1521—and it may well belong to about 1540, to judge by the type of music contained in it. An interesting feature of this manuscript is the occurrence of certain rhythmic trends that become typical of much virginal music of a later period, e.g.

[1] Strype, the historian, says that Philip came on horseback to St. Paul's to hear a Mass performed, and probably composed, by Spaniards on Oct. 18th, 1554. Stowe writes—'At this tyme ther was so many Spanyards in London that a man shoulde have mett in the stretes for one Inglishman above iiij Spanyards . . .' (Harl. 419.).

I   B.K.M.

Ex. LXXV (A Hornepype)

These dance rhythms are noticeable also in the serious work of Tallis (Felix Namque, 1562) as well as in Byrd and later composers; which may point to certain individual developments in English keyboard music. Of equal interest to the 'Hornpype' are the more or less similar compositions, 'My Ladye Wynkfyld's Rounde' and 'My Ladye Carey's Dumpe'.

There is no doubt that there was an extensive body of organ composers in England during the first half of the sixteenth century, as witness the famous Mulliner Book (Brit. Mus. Add. 30513) and other manuscripts in the British Museum (Add. 29996 and 15233), as well as in the libraries of Christ Church, the Bodleian and others. The first is a large collection of organ works, probably for practical use at old St. Paul's Cathedral, where Thomas Mulliner was choirmaster. All this consists of works on sacred and secular canti-firmi, like many of the period, some in a rather stolid note-against-note counterpoint, and others in a more florid technique, such as the major works of John Redford (c. 1485-c. 1547), Blytheman (d. 1591) and Tallis (c. 1510-1585). Some are small imitational pieces with 'means' (middle parts) or 'poynts' (counterpoints), while others again have considerable developments, such as the arrangements of 'Felix Namque' by Farrant and Shelbye, as well as the various 'Gloria Tibi Trinitas' (In Nomine) settings by Blytheman. (The first-mentioned theme was frequently used with great elaboration by later writers. See Tallis's example in Fitzwilliam Book, Bk. 1, 427.) The pieces by Redford predominate, followed by Tallis and Blytheman, the younger members of the school.

Redford's works appear the most developed, interesting though some of Blytheman's pieces are. It is possible that Redford was followed by Thomas Mulliner as organist of St. Paul's, and that Mulliner made this collection after his predecessor's death or retirement. It is said that (John) Sheppard, another composer represented in this manuscript, was educated by Mulliner at St. Paul's, so that this group of organists may well be called the 'St. Paul's' organ school.[1] Redford's predominance can also be seen in the fact that he apparently monopolizes Add. 15233. These pieces are more ornate than the Mulliner works, and may be for solo performance. The Add. 29996, a very extensive book, is for practical use again, and contains numerous short organ settings of the service, as well as some more elaborate ones. A large number, again, are in only two parts, with a melismatic flow of quavers over a steady movement in minims, which is frequently reminiscent of the German organists of the fifteenth century, and may mean that the old English organ music is older in origin than the contemporary European schools. Though most of the works in the manuscripts are somewhat severe, at their best they have a dignity and grace, combined with deep feeling, that make them worthy of more study and performance than have hitherto been given them by English musicians.

Before entering on the later Elizabethan period mention should be made of the neglected keyboard music of Tallis and Blytheman, whose works came out in about 1560–70. Technically these composers were very well equipped, as can be seen from Blytheman's 'In Nomine' and Tallis's 'Felix Namque' settings (1562–4). In the two Tallis arrangements great rhythmic variety is used. Both may have been played in a vigorous harpsichord style not unlike that of Bull's compositions. (See Ex. LXVI.)

As keyboard composers Tallis and Blytheman need reconsideration. English scholars who have found them dull were unfamiliar with pre-Elizabethan keyboard music. Whatever contrary opinion

[1] Philyppe Apprys, another composer in Add. 29996 (Brit. Mus.), was also at St. Paul's.

Ex. LXXVI (Felix Namque)

has been held, the pieces named were probably written for the virginal or kindred instruments.

Whatever the influences, the fact is that, after the austere counterpoint of the mid-sixteenth-century organists, the English from the time of Byrd onwards (c. 1580) developed an individual style of their own which amounted to an English keyboard renaissance; for around Byrd a group of virginal composers arose, such as Thomas Morley (c. 1545–1604) and Giles Farnaby (c. 1560–1620), whose school flourished down to the time of the Puritan ascendency, and was by no means extinguished even then. The bulk of this music is contained in one of the most amazing collections known to history, namely the 'Fitzwilliam Virginal Book', which contains 297 examples ranging from about 1580 to about 1612. Preceding this, there are : a large manuscript book entitled 'My Ladye Nevell's Booke' (1591), which apparently is all by Byrd (42 pieces); the famous printed work for virginal, 'Parthenia' (1611), stated to be the first, by Byrd, Bull and Gibbons; and 'Benjamin Cosyn's Book' (c. 1600–1610), which also contains works by Byrd, Bull and others (98 pieces). There are also later volumes like 'Will Foster's Book' (1624), as well as other unnamed manuscripts in the various libraries of England, Europe and America.[1]

It is interesting to note the predominance of hand-written

[1] For complete list of Byrd's compositions and their manuscripts consult: Fellowes (E. H.), *William Byrd* (Oxf. Univ. Press), 1948. Manuscripts containing Dr. John Bull's keyboard works will be found in Glyn (Margaret), *John Bull*, Vol. I, (Preface) (Stainer & Bell), 1928. For still further information the

material in England as against printed works in Italy. The same applies to the music of the Netherlands and parts of Germany. Most of the works written out belong to a noticeably earlier date than the manuscripts. Whether they were intended for organ or harpsichord has to be guessed—rather by the secular nature of the pieces than by the titles.[1] A deduction is that much music printed abroad may, in spite of the frequent sub-title 'organ and other keyed instruments', equally be considered as harpsichord music. The keyboard manuscripts of Europe are still largely unexplored.

The music of the Elizabethan virginalist as exemplified by the above works consisted mostly of dances, dance variations and variations on popular or quasi-popular airs. Of these there are some particularly delightful examples that can take their stand with anything yet written at the time:

Ex. LXXVIIa (Callino Casturame. Byrd)

Ex. LXXVIIb (Tower Hill. Farnaby)

Byrd's dance pieces, like those of Farnaby and others, enchant us with their tunefulness and are full of that charm and character which we recognise as Elizabethan. The historian must at the same time insist that this late English Renaissance had had almost a cen-

reader should consult authorities like Naylor, Anderton, Glyn and Fellowes, and especially the article on virginal music in Grove's Dictionary. See Bibliography at the end of this work (p. 151).

[1] It is possible, of course, that many dances were also adapted for organ use. Bull's 'Pavana of my Lord Lumley', for instance, is perfectly suitable for the modern organ. Note also the inclusion of dances in the tablatures of Ammerbach and Kotter (pp. 46-7 and 43).

tury of Continental forerunners. The Italians had been composing gracious dance music since Dalza (1508) or earlier, and there are some attractive dances in Bendusi (1553) as well as by the German Ammerbach (1571) and Normiger (1598). The dance pieces of the English, however, have an open, natural style of phrasing which gives them a tunefulness in advance of the Continent, and it is not too much to say of the melodies of the later Elizabethans that they have a strength of character comparable with the poetry of the period.

Byrd's variations are full of technical resource, invention and variety. If he did not develop his themes and forms as did some of the Italians, and occasionally adopted the rather rustic drone-like accompaniments typical of much English virginal music, his variety was inspired by musical reasons rather than by mere technical ingenuity. Byrd as a keyboard composer charms posterity by the sweetness of his melody and the freshness of his inspiration. We should not judge him with national bias, as an isolated figure, without regard for the brilliant achievements on the Continent; for though it is true that the Italians clung to a quasi-ecclesiastical smoothness of style in their themes, in their finest polyphony and the best examples of their instrumental forms, such as Merulo's toccatas and the younger Gabrieli's canzoni, they achieved a brilliance of style that was to have much effect on the future. But Byrd will always remain outstanding—a man of genius—whose fecundity and musical gifts will be a constant wonder and pleasure to future generations.

Of very nearly equal melodic power was Giles Farnaby. He possessed fine musicianship and a keen sense of phrase, as witness his 'Quodlings Delight', 'Daphne', 'Put up thy dagger Jenny', and other variations. His melodies have a rustic sweetness, and there is wonderful aspiration in such pieces as his famous 'Toye' dance. That he had a fine keyboard technique can be seen from his 'King's Hunt', 'Bony Sweet Robin' and the variations on 'Wooddy-Cock', where broken octaves and repeated notes are used in a way more often thought of in connection with Bull. In date Farnaby lies between Byrd and Bull, but his musicianship is quite up to that of Bull's period.

The Elizabethans were also capable of excellent polyphony, as witness their numerous fantasias or fancies. The Northern European 'fantasia' became almost a type in English keyboard and instrumental music, more or less equivalent to the Italian ricercar, though generally much freer than the compact and learned composition of the Italians. The use of the term 'fantasia' became looser towards the end of the sixteenth century. It generally referred to any imitative composition with fugal entries of one or more subjects, without the development of the later fugue. The rather similar though older forms on canti-firmi and themes like the 'In Nomine' were also still employed, where great skill in modulation was shown, as in the following section from Byrd's hexachordal fantasia:

Ex. LXXVIII (Fantasia 'Ut, re, mi, fa, sol, la')

also:

Ex. LXXIX (ibid.)

The English also cultivated the short keyboard 'praeludium'—a prelude in the true sense of the word—more akin to the early German preambulum than the formal Italian toccata. One of the best examples of this type can be seen in Bull's Praeludium in the Fitzwilliam Book II, p. 22 (Fuller-Maitland & Barclay Squire edition).

The third period of English keyboard music began more or less with the accession of James I, with the music of Dr. John Bull (1563–1628), the later works of Farnaby, and Peter Philips (c. 1560–c. 1633), though the last-named spent much of his life abroad. This school presents great technical developments and an expansion of material on lines similar to those of the Netherlanders. Thus much of the typically English passage-work, broken chords, reiterated notes and other ornamentations, is also to be found in Sweelinck, though they developed in a more individual style with the later English. Some have held that our country had a good deal to do with this technical progress in the Netherlands. But it is also arguable that the English virginalists may have been influenced by musicians like Sweelinck rather than the other way about. This question of give and take is complicated. The Netherlands possibly had a closer connection than we with the Italian musical Renaissance, and Sweelinck, if never actually at Venice, had before 1581 submitted to Venetian influence. He had already a great reputation, let us remember, before the English compositions were circulated on the Continent, as a contemporary epitaph tells us:

> 'Joanis Petrus Sweelingeris Amsterdamus
> Cujus fama Italos tegigit salsosque Britannos,
> Quique, Orlande, tuis notus erat Bavaris
> Omnibus ex terris peregrinus trexerat aures.'

Not that the circulation of manuscripts is evidence, since it was common to all European countries throughout the sixteenth century.

Peter Philips was organist at Antwerp from about 1596, and later at Brussels, but to judge by the date of his major compositions in the Fitzwilliam Book (1592–93–95, etc.) he must have been writing virginal music before his final settlement in the Netherlands. John Bull toured the Netherlands and other parts of Northern Europe in 1601. He returned to England shortly afterwards but went to the Continent again in 1613, where he became organist at Brussels and later at Antwerp (1617), remaining in that post until his death. The last date in the Fitzwilliam Book is 1612. Bull was fifty then, so that he evidently developed his keyboard work in England (seven of his pieces occur in the 'Parthenia' of 1611). Other Englishmen were in the Netherlands, where they had taken refuge on religious grounds. The compiler of the Fitzwilliam Book was certainly familiar with Catholics in the Netherlands, and apparently admired Sweelinck's works. But the general evidence is that the English developed a style of their own in spite of their repeated contacts with the Flemings and Dutch. There is still room, however, for investigation into Northern European harpsichord music.

More interesting than the question of influences is the quality of the music produced. The English composers had a character of their own, and their keyboard music has a value transcending all talk about sources. John Bull was a man of genius, both as an executive virtuoso and composer. Peter Philips too was an excellent musician. Judging by his transcriptions he must have been aware of his Italian contemporaries, but his style is individual and distinctly English. He had a good sense for form and phrase, with a feeling for harmonic movement. Technically he was very well developed and had a skill not far off Bull's.

Bull's inventive power as a performer, however, was prodigious, and was only to be rivalled by Frescobaldi in the following generation. In his variations and other works he displays a unique keyboard sense, not by mere virtuosity, but by his feeling as a performer. His music reveals a strong personality, with a style that is virile and masterly. For evidence of his great musicianship, both executive and creative, witness his variations on the 'Quodran Pavan', the 'Washingham' air, the 'Pavana of my Lord Lumley' and 'Galiard' to the Pavan No. 33 (Fitzwilliam). In his contrapuntal works he showed great ingenuity, as can be seen in his hexachordal

fantasia, 'ut re mi fa sol la', and the excellent capriccio on a theme
by Sweelinck.

Ex. LXXX

His dance music has rare quality, with broad and wayward melodies that suggest the adventurousness of his age. Bull was a master,
and his imaginative powers are comparable only with those of
his illustrious friend Pieterszoon Sweelinck.

The English school was by now superior to all in Europe outside Italy, and to peruse the massive volumes of the modern reprint of the Fitzwilliam Book is to be amazed by the strength and
spirit of the English virginalists at the end of Elizabeth's reign.
Even now they are too little appreciated. Byrd's brilliant and
refreshing variations on the 'Sellenger's Round', with its wonderful sense of phrase and harmony, and Bull's virile and exhilarating
variations on the 'King's Hunt' are among examples of keyboard
music that deserve to live forever in the minds of men. Only the
religious strife of the seventeenth century prevented this school
from developing on lines corresponding to those of the
Continental schools.

Before leaving this wonderful era, we may touch upon one of
England's greatest musicians, though by date he belongs to

another age. Orlando Gibbons (1583–1625) died when he was 42, and as a musician is Jacobean. His compositions reveal the coming of a new generation, with his melodies noticeably simpler in pattern and smoother in style than those of the surviving Elizabethans. Musically he is often superior to them, and his counterpoint moves with a grace that savours of the baroque period. He wrote some delightful dance pieces, but his genius is best expressed in the contrapuntal works such as the 'Fantasia of four parts' or the 'Fantasia for double organ', where his dignified contemplativeness finds an apter medium. In spirit he is reminiscent of Frescobaldi and might well be considered as the English rival of that master. He had a deep sense of harmony, which was the expression of a mellow intelligence and feeling, while the variety of his technique as expressed in his variations on 'Hunts up or Pescod time', the 'Woods soe wilde' and the 'Lord Salisbury's Pavan', show the power of his musicianship. The same can be said of his excellent galliards and pavans.[1] As a composer of both keyboard and other instrumental music he is one of the finest England has yet produced, both by force of his skill and the dignity of his grace and character.

[1] See Margaret Glyn's *Orlando Gibbons*, Vol. I, Preface (1925), for a complete list of his works and manuscripts.

Chapter IX

THE BEGINNINGS OF THE BAROQUE KEYBOARD SCHOOLS

Girolamo Frescobaldi

Frescobaldi, one of the greatest musicians of the seventeenth century, was born at Ferrara in 1583. He was a pupil of Luzzasco Luzzaschi, and is said also to have studied under the French composer Milleville.

Ferrara in the light of modern research appears to have been a city of high musical importance. Obrecht, Brumel and Josquin resided there in various musical capacities. In 1586, three years after Frescobaldi's birth, the Duke of Ferrara possessed one of the largest and best orchestras in Europe.

Frescobaldi played the organ in his native town for a time, and spent some of his student days in Flanders (1608), where he may have observed some Spanish as well as Flemish trends. It is not likely that he came into touch with Sweelinck, but perhaps he heard Peter Philips play at Antwerp. At St. Peter's, Rome, in that same year, when he was 25, Baini says that thirty thousand people came to hear him perform. He retained the position of organist there—save for a break in the years 1628–1633, when he was at Florence—until his death.

Frescobaldi's art as an organist was striking and far-reaching in effect. He raised organ technique to a standard never previously attained, and seems to have possessed an imaginativeness above any other keyboard artist in Europe. We must suppose there was magnetism in his personality, like that which Liszt and Paderewski exerted over recent generations, and many stories circulated about his character and performance. His technique was probably exceptional, for his style is fine and fanciful, and he must have had original ideas of fingering, since his passage-work is both well phrased and expressive. As with most of his contemporaries,

the melodic interest of his work lay in the semiquaver movement, but with Frescobaldi this was carried to a greater degree of
subtlety.

His reputation was founded not only on his virtuosity, but also
on the extraordinary imaginativeness of his compositions. This
sometimes rose to mystic heights. The strange poetry of his music
sprang from an unusual temperament. This is indicated in the
prefaces he wrote for his works, which we are lucky in possessing, for they tell us something about the man's mind, as well as
giving clues to the technique of the period. 'Whosoever can understand me, let him do so. I understand myself,' he writes in the
introduction to one of his works.

In his harmony he seems to touch upon many keys in the
modern sense, although it is clear he was working on modal principles. At moments we feel we are in C, D, E, F, G, or A, major
or minor, and there are allusions to E♭, A♭ and B minor tonalities.
Even a bold F minor or D♭ major chord can be descried. In many
respects Frescobaldi may be considered as one of the pioneers
modern tonality. Again and again his modulations point to future
developments. Church organist though he was, it is possible that
the operatic works performed at Rome and Florence at the time
did not escape him.

What such a master as Frescobaldi lacked in the way of latter-
day harmonic resource he made up for in suspensions,[1] and by
this method Frescobaldi used both the dominant and diminished
7th, and even 9ths, most freely: e.g.

Ex. LXXXI (Toccata No. 10. 1614)

Occasionally he reaches such daring harmonies as (See Ex.
LXXXII):

[1] See p. 70.

Ex. LXXXII

and had a taste for queer intervals like:

Ex. LXXXIII

Frescobaldi's chromaticism was even more acute than Sweelinck's, and as a contemporary said of one of his publications, 'his
music bristles with black notes.' An example of his chromatic harmony is the entire section of the above-mentioned Passacaglia.
His genius for counterpoint, chromatic and otherwise, places him
as the chief forerunner of the still greater art of Sebastian Bach.
He was the most subtle composer of his day and, along with Froberger and Buxtehude, probably the greatest keyboard musician of
the seventeenth century.

I have said that we get hints of the originality of the man in his
prefaces. More than once he recommends the use of 'tempo
rubato.' Thus:

> 'Some trills and tender passages must be played adagio some-
> what extending the bar, although a toccata can be played accord-
> ing to the fancy of the performer.' (Fiori Musicali, 1635.)

Again in the Toccatas of the 1614 edition he mentions 'the kind
of style' that must not be subject to time, but:

> 'beaten now slowly, now quickly, and even held in the air.'
> 'On the last note of the shakes or passages . . . you must pause.'
> 'At the end of the passages or cadences you must retard the time
> more and more.' 'The notes of a shake are not all equal, but are

to be given with more expression than rapidity.' 'Pause slightly before beginning a passage with both hands.' 'Cadences must be sustained before taking the normal movement.' 'It is often convenient to soften certain dissonances by means of rallentando and arpeggiando.' . . . 'In any case I leave it to the judgment of the student.'[1] And again: 'The opening of every toccata may be played adagio, although composed in quavers, and then, according to the passage, more allegro'. (Fiori Musicali.)

In the Capriccios (1624) he advises us to

'Start adagio so that what follows can be brought into greater relief.'

The word 'adagio' must here be understood with a looser meaning than to-day (i.e. not so slow). He urged the pupil to study a score before beginning to play it, and to recommence at the same place where he had left off instead of going back to the beginning again.

His forms are as advanced as they are resourceful. The ricercari and fantasias have all the learning of the earlier masters, together with an expanded development, while the toccatas, partitas, capriccios and canzonas are full of new variety, inventiveness and expression. The first toccatas were shaped somewhat on the sixteenth-century model, but in the later examples a completely free and individual conception was attained.

The canzonas are divided into sections of contrasting character, with frequent changes from duple to triple time, or vice-versa. The main theme which forms the basis of each section is altered with such cunning that it is not always easy to trace at a glance. In the 3rd canzona in the 1627 edition of his toccatas, for instance, the primary theme is varied as follows:

[1] In the 1614 edition of the Toccatas again, he says that 'the beginning of a toccata must be adagio and arpeggiando', and that the 'syncopations of discords' can occur in the middle of a piece. This shows how much must have been left to the fancy of the executant. The arpeggiation of chords probably occurred in cembalo playing rather than on the organ, which presumably followed the already ornate printed versions.

Ex. LXXXIV

In each section the varied theme is given a new series of entries, as if to form a fresh composition.

In the Capriccio, the theme, taken from the bass of another composition, and often used in close conjunction with a series of countersubjects, is frequently employed in augmentation or diminution, now in one voice, now in another, forming sections in new counterpoint like the canzon, save that alternation of rhythms is not necessarily adopted. In both these compositions each section shows an amazing variety both of mood and texture.

The partitas are true variations, and here Frescobaldi displays extraordinary ingenuity in contrasting rhythm and varying polyphony. Many of the themes derive from well-known dances, like the 'Bergamasca' or 'La Follia', or else from the works of contemporary composers. Frescobaldi also used melodies based on the notes of the cuckoo or suggested by the noises of battle—both of which were popular subjects with composers of his own and succeeding generations. ·

Last but not least are the dance pieces for cembalo. For pure melody, grace, dignity and fineness of phrasing, nothing in the whole period is more artistically contrived than Frescobaldi's dance music. It may be placed alongside that of Bach and Handel and should count among the classics of their kind. This music has a strong harmonic basis and is interwoven with delicate counterpoint. The forms mostly used were the Corrento, Galliardo, Balletto and Passacaglia.

Frescobaldi's sense of development and polyphonic structure can be perceived in any number of examples. The 'Toccata on the 6th tone', for instance, from the 1614 edition of his toccatas, a composition built upon imitative and florid passage-work, is an excellent illustration, full of spirit, with great expressiveness in the

PLATE XII

PAGE FROM THE FIRST TOCCATA
From the Toccatas of Girolamo Frescobaldi

GIROLAMO FRESCOBALDI
From the Frontispiece of the Toccatas

semiquaver movement. The middle section, calm and contrasting, is not so highly developed as some of the latter toccatas, but the more florid passages have a greater subtlety of detail than the toccatas of the Merulo order.

Ex. LXXXV (Toccata No. 10. 1614)

In the following toccata from the 1627 edition the movement is carried far beyond the Venetian variety. The passage-work is better phrased and is more akin to the style of Bach which, indeed, in the first section it prematurely follows.

Ex. LXXXVI (Toccata in G minor)

It flows with the greatest ease, and with that intensity and expressiveness typical of Frescobaldi's art. The second section, which acts as a bridge, is filled with one of his characteristically contemplative moods.

Ex. LXXXVII

The next section forms a contrast, with a semi-rhythmic movement built on a simple motif. The following section, with a graceful flow of quavers, affords another contrast, preceded by a

K   B.K.M.

rallentando which illustrates Frescobaldi's frequent use of the rhetorical pause.

Ex. LXXXVIII

The next part again is very expressive, reaching a degree of intensity that can only be described as genius.

Ex. LXXXIX

The following movement, with characteristic triplets, is skilfully composed in a then advanced form of three-part counterpoint.

Ex. XC

The finale is another example of Frescobaldi's power and grandeur. And this is far from being the only composition of its kind.

The canzona from the 1627 edition, given below, with its typical sections of alternating time-signatures, is another example of the master's workmanship. It is based on a single subject, which is varied and rearranged with striking skill, as shown on page 128. The first section continues as follows:

Ex. XCI (Canzon No. 3 in G)

Attention may be drawn to the noble pathos of the second portion, and to its clever weaving of the parts.

Ex. XCII

This strange and sad expression is carried on with even greater art in the following section, where quaint harmonies are arrived at by a cunning arrangement of the theme: (See also Ex. LXXXIII.)

Ex. XCIII

Attention should also be paid to the skill and expressiveness of the third and fourth sections. (See Ex. XCIV.)

A bridge, with an expressive bass, leads to a contrapuntal finale in flowing style. It is based on the original theme, though cleverly disguised, and has a counter-subject which begins before the first subject, and carries on in quasi-ricercar style.

The 1st corrento from the 1614 edition is the best known of Frescobaldi's compositions and one of the most graceful compositions he ever wrote. Half a page in length and perfect in form,

Ex. XCIV

one could not wish for a note more or less. What could be more nobly conceived than this passage in the second half of the composition?

Ex. XCV (Corrente, No. 1)

A treasure from a mind second to none at the time it was written.

The following corrento is equally well phrased and is graced with a beautiful melody. It affords an example of Frescobaldi's genius for modulation.

Ex. XCVI (Corrento del Balletto)

The preceding passacaglia is a rhythmic dance on a ground-bass which, in spite of a certain gaiety, is strongly coloured by that subtle melancholy which pervades most of Frescobaldi's music. Its rhythmic figures are as gracefully patterned as an eighteenth-century minuet, and the quaver passages

Ex. XCVII (Passacaglia)

show what an excellent clavier technique he must have possessed. The masterly last section has a striking harmonic interest with its diminished 7ths and 9ths.

Ex. XCVIII

Frescobaldi's music is too little appreciated, despite the recognition he gets in the history books. The average organist who thinks of him as drily learned is mistaken. Frescobaldi's counterpoint is expressive to the point of mysticism. If we find true consolation in the style of Bach, then Frescobaldi too has much to give us. His colour is entirely his own, which gives added pleasure to those who already love the rich texture of the polyphonic age. We delight in the gifts of other musicians of this period, but here in Frescobaldi is true genius. These toccatas, partitas, capriccios and canzonas have only to be played to be acclaimed.

Frescobaldi had many pupils, the chief of them being J. J. Froberger (1600–1667) and possibly Michelangelo Rossi (1600–c.1670), apart from his basic influence on the South German schools.

His numerous compositions ran in his own time into many editions. The principal ones are:

Il Primo Libro di Madrigali à 5 voci, 1608 (Vocal).

Il Primo Libro delle Fantasie à 4, 1608.

Toccate e Partite d'Intavolatura di Cimbalo (et Organo), 1614–15–16–27–37. (Primo Libro.)

Recercari et Canzoni Franzesi (Rome), 1615–18–26–45.

Il Primo Libro delle Canzoni, 1623–28–34 (35 Instumental pieces). (The 1628 edition contains 2 toccatas, one for spinet or lute, the other for violino and spinet, or violino and lute.)

Il Primo Libro di Capricci fatti sopra diversi soggetti (Rome), 1624. (Venice), 1626–27–28–42–45.

Il Secundo Libro di Toccate . . . (Rome), (1626)–1627–28–37. (1627 edition contains canzoni, versi and Magnificats, etc. (1637), Primo and Secundo Libro together.)

Il Primo Libro d'Arie Musicali (Florence), 1630. Songs with gravicembalo and theorbo (bass lute).

Fiori Musicali (Rome), 1635.

(See Eitner's Quellen-Lexicon for MSS. Keyboard and Instrumental works.)

GENERAL TENDENCIES AFTER THE SWEELINCK AND FRESCOBALDI PERIODS

In the age following Frescobaldi we find a division of the German organ school into north and south. Both derived from Italy, and the north also from Sweelinck. Schütz and Hassler were pupils of Giovanni and Andrea Gabrieli, and Samuel Scheidt and Scheidemann (1596–1663) were Sweelinck's most famous pupils. Scheidemann was the master of Reinken, who in his turn directly influenced Sebastian Bach.

Frescobaldi taught J. J. Froberger (c. 1600–1667) and perhaps Michelangelo Rossi (c. 1600–c. 1670) who, through Kaspar Kerll (1627–1693), Pasquini (1637–1710) and Georg Muffat (c. 1645–1704)—whose compositions had a formative effect upon Handel —completed the South German schools. Buxtehude belonged to the North German school; Pachelbel came between the two.

There is another influence, that of the French school, whose wealth of harmony and stylized forms had much effect in Europe.

The English, although not uninfluenced by the Continent, maintained their open, natural style, which is best described as a broad melodiousness.

Most of these musicians are outside the scope of this work. An exception is Samuel Scheidt (1587–1654). His work represents the development of elements derived from Sweelinck. He composed toccatas, fantasias and canzoni, but his most noteworthy contributions to the keyboard are his variations on psalms, chorales and songs, in which he showed great resource and inventive ability. The ideas came from Sweelinck, but these were developed on a more extended scale, with a more melodious treatment of variations, which are solid, well harmonized pieces and show a more modern feeling for variety than Frescobaldi's polyphonic variations. Scheidt's technique is remarkable, particularly in his invention of effects. In this he much resembles John Bull, though the effects are generally more advanced. His 'Tabulatura Nova' (1624), which marks an epoch in organ playing, is one of the first collections to contain an independent pedal part. His organ at Halle, which was said to be the best of its time, is specified on p. 70-1.

The Renaissance is by now in the past. We are in the midst of the seventeenth century, that is to say, on the threshold of the high Baroque. It may be said that Sweelinck and Frescobaldi belong to this age rather than to the Renaissance, but they have been appended here as representing, in some of their aspects, a culmination of effects adumbrated in the earlier sixteenth century. It will have been appreciated that 'Renaissance' is a term used in this book in a special musical sense. In general European culture and the other arts the Renaissance had set in before this. There are no hard and fast lines to be drawn in artistic history.

CHAPTER X

THE TECHNIQUE OF EARLY KEYBOARD MUSIC

The finger technique of the fifteenth and earlier centuries is an obscure subject, and any light that can be thrown upon it is valuable in helping us to form a proper conception and interpretation of that early music.

In the fourteenth and fifteenth centuries the thumb and 1st finger, or 1st and 2nd together, are said to have been used in moving from one note of a scale to another on the 'organum magnum'.[1] On the smaller organs the middle fingers were the ones mainly used. The following example, quoted from Arnold Schering's 'Geschichte der Musik in Beispielen', shows the method at the time of Hans Buchner's 'Fundamentum' (*c.* 1513).

Ex. XCIX (Buchner. Quem terra pontus)

The Spanish organist Bermudo (*c.* 1510–1560) in his 'Declaracion' (1549) gives the following curious fingering for the scale:

Ex. C

---

[1] Grove's Dict. Article on 'Fingering'.

According to Ammerbach, in 1571 the scale was fingered:

Ex. CI

Major thirds were taken by the 2nd and 4th fingers; intervals up to a sixth by the 2nd and 5th, e.g.

Ex. CII

the thumb being used only for intervals over a 6th as in an octave. In fact the thumb and little finger were rarely used, save in the left hand and for stretching intervals as above.

On the early portative the hand was often held sideways or, if parallel, a trifle low, the three middle fingers doing most of the work, and this may account for the above-mentioned fingering. Many instruments, like the cembalo and portative organ, were frequently placed on a table, and to judge by the paintings of the day the hands usually lay quite neatly over the keys. Thumbs are depicted as hanging away from the keyboard. Sometimes the wrists drop a little, but in a self-portrait of a lady in 1543,[1] the hands are quite well arched. In the earliest paintings and sculptures of players, the hand is often depicted as lying well over the keyboard.

Merulo's fingering according to Diruta was:

Ex. CIII

[1] See Kinsky's *A History of Music in Pictures*, 'Catharina van Hemessen'.

but he states that many famous players ascended on 1st and 2nd and descended on 3rd and 4th. Most of the passage-work was done by the three middle fingers, i.e.:

Ex. CIV

but the thumb seems to have played a certain part in the left hand, and in some instances in the right; as we see in some examples from Ammerbach and Merulo:

Ex. CV

The thumb was of course allowed in leaps (see p. 84) and for intervals over a fourth (in Merulo's case)

Ex. CVI

The English virginalist of a later period (John Bull, etc.) used both the thumb and little finger for the scale:

Ex. CVII

and it is more than possible that fine players like G. Gabrieli, Sweelinck and Frescobaldi adopted a similar practice. (Examples taken from Dolmetsch, A., *The Interpretation of the Music of the XVIIth and XVIIIth Centuries,* 1915.)

This awkward-seeming method of going up in 3 and 4, or 3 and 2, and coming down in 3 and 2 or 3 and 4, remained in vogue until the end of the seventeenth century, e.g.

Ex. CVIII

and can be traced in many of the later masters, including Bach himself, who constantly passed the third over the fourth finger.

This old style of fingering is not so difficult as it looks, and with practice produces quite smooth results. But semiquavers cannot be played at a modern allegro tempo by this old fingering; and this fact makes us realize that most compositions of that period were probably played four times as slowly as one is inclined to perform them. Not an unimportant fact to remember! That there was some diversity of opinion is indicated by Michael Praetorius' 'Syntagma Musicum' (1619):

> 'Many think it is a matter of great importance, and despise such organists as do not use this or that particular fingering, which in my opinion is not worth the talk; for let a player run up or down with first or middle or third finger, ay, even with his nose, if that could help him, provided everything is done clearly, correctly, and gracefully . . .'

It is noteworthy that a much more correct interpretation can be obtained if the old technique is used. It automatically gives an accent in keeping with the passage-work of the time, which forms groups of two rather than of four notes, as seen in the following:

Ex. CIX

This sub-division may help us to understand what Frescobaldi and other musicians of the seventeenth and early eighteenth centuries meant about the unequal duration of accented and unaccented quavers and semiquavers, thus:

Ex. CX

The second example represents the commoner practice. Frescobaldi says that the second note was 'somewhat dotted'; Couperin that the first was 'a very little dotted'. One writer of the eighteenth century asserts that the first note in such a group of two varied from 1/2 to 2/3, 3/5 or 5/7 of the value of the next, but that much was left to taste. This inequality of duration of quavers and semiquavers written as equal prevailed in music for other instruments and for voices; and hence it may be that keyboard fingering was designed to agree with a general practice of rhythm and accent.

In the barring of sixteenth-century keyboard music, the measure (bar) was usually twice the length of ours. Thus instead of a 4/4 bar, one of 4/2 time is found, grouping thirty-two semiquavers in four groups of eight, e.g.

Ex. CXI

Ex. CXII usually edited as:

but better as:

Phrasing and accent in the sixteenth century were subtle, and if attention is not paid to it the passage-work will often appear

meaningless, as it has frequently been accused of being. This particularly applies to Merulo and the elder Gabrieli. It must be remembered that their notions of scale movement were probably
derived from vocal music, in which each note was articulated
with the utmost distinctness. The use of a mere rush of scales as
passage-work belongs to the eighteenth century, and is among
the features differentiating the polyphonic from the classical
schools.

A difficult question is that of the right tempo to adopt in early
keyboard music. If taken as slowly as the practice of the time seems
to have been, the movement runs the danger of becoming dull.
A quicker tempo gives us a brighter performance, but the danger
of an anachronistic interpretation is incurred. The rhythm of sixteenth-century music is still rather that of stress and continued
motion than one aware of the division of the bar-line, though the
desire, at least from the Merulo age, for a mensural beat seems
ever present. Quasi-adagio and andante tempos are the most
appropriate for the sixteenth and seventeenth century organ compositions. It must be remembered that both harpsichord and organ
can do with a slower pace than the modern pianoforte, without a
sense of dragging.

The first principle is to pay attention to the expression of the
parts. The passage-work contains most of the melody, whether it
be the plainsong-like melisma of the Paumann age or the florid
drapery of the Venetian toccata. When the interpreter has been
urged to remember what was the spirit of the age and the stately
and splendid surroundings of this music when it was new, much
must still be left to his taste and judgment. As for phrasing and
accent, he must take into account the changes that have supervened
since the period of our discussion. In the earlier sixteenth-century
music we may frequently phrase a passage thus:

Ex. CXIII

while later on the same notes may be rendered:

Ex. CXIV

Much has been made about the ornamentation of the early key-board and other music. In the main it seems that ornamentation was reserved for the harpsichord and clavichord rather than the organ. Diruta states that in playing 'quilled' instruments, 'tremoli' and 'accenti' could be used for the longer notes (Il Transilvano, 1597). In the case of the organ, however, it seems that the music was normally read as written. It is unlikely, on the other hand, that much could have been added to Merulo's and others' figuration even on the harpsichord. It seems that a great deal was left to taste, for the examples given by the authorities show such variety that nothing but the keenest discrimination could have said when and where they should have been used. It is doubtful whether they were employed for all occasions. Diruta's illustrations for such figures as

Ex. CXV

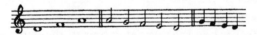

would have ended in mere chaos unless selected by careful judgment. Note, for instance, his interpretation of the Groppo, Tremolo and Tremoletto (half shake):

Ex. CXVI

Dannreuther's Musical Ornamentation. Part I.)

Even the older Ammerbach tablature (1571) shows something the same for the Mordant:

Ex. CXVII

Diruta says that the speed of the Tremoli ran from 'slow' to those of 'lightness and agility'. If we remember the fingering and the general tempo of the compositions of that time, which was never much above Andante for semiquavers, we can imagine the rate of movement for such ornamentations as:

Ex. CXVIII

Considering the commonplace nature of the above figures before elaboration, it seems that most ornamentation of the sixteenth century was purely a personal matter, to be used only at suitable moments or cadences. The possible variety of Accenti on two notes as illustrated by Praetorius, show the kind of attitude taken:

Ex. CXIX

With the later Northern European and English composers, certain ornaments formulated into true graces:

Ex. CXX

This was the same with the seventeenth-century writers of France and Germany, when there was a constant attempt to group the endless variety of ornaments into a single system. Early Italian ornamentation, on the other hand, was more in the nature of passage-work than mere graces. A study of their written music will show a student how best this is to be performed. As a whole, a normal reading of the score will suffice for the organ or piano, with only an occasional use of a groppo or tremolo for the harpsichord.[1]

This music is best performed on an organ or harpsichord. The pianoforte is inappropriate, only to be used with discrimination for practical purposes. Some works are specifically for organ, such as the tablatures of Paumann, Schlick and Hofhaimer, and the printed volumes of Buus, Cavazzoni and Merulo. But many pieces were applicable to either harpsichord or organ. Such are most of the works of Andrea and Giovanni Gabrieli and of Frescobaldi, though the organ is really the better suited to them. The colouring of all this music was infinitely different from modern lusciousness, and always to be borne in mind is the nasal tone of those old organs and the twang of the lutes and harpsichords, as well as the gruffness of Renaissance wind-bands of trombones and shawms. The charm of that colouring will be the more appreciated the more it is known, and it will be no unimportant factor in the pleasure that will be derived from this music in the days when it is once more given its due. Excessive adaptation of the mere notes to what may be imagined as modern requirements would mean its death once and for all.

Renaissance music and medieval music are worth retrieving. Those were great ages of European culture, and their music was

[1] For an extended study of the sixteenth and seventeenth century ornament the reader should turn to the above-mentioned authority, as well as to Arnold Dolmetsch's work quoted on page 139.

worthy of them. It is naive to regard those musicians as restricted by the simplicity of their equipment. Are Giotto and Botticelli considered to have been so handicapped? An artist's restrictions are the making of his art. I have endeavoured to indicate some of the individual characteristics of the great men whose legacy the world of to-day still ignores—the bitter-sweet qualities of the fifteenth-century organists—Schlick's austerity and dignity—Hofhaimer's warmth—the rich texture of the Italian composers—Claudio Merulo's poetic individuality—the brilliant melodiousness of the Gabrielis—as well as the fine, hard quality of the northern Sweelinck—the pleasing and broader tunefulness of the English musicians, and that amazing compound of learning and imagination, Girolamo Frescobaldi. Only naive inexperience and ignorance will dismiss them as merely archaic, superseded and monotonous. Those men created wonderful things. Forgotten they are by the world, but not lost. Their revival will extend the boundaries of our pleasures and add to the glories we know of the world of beauty.

SELECTED BIBLIOGRAPHY
INCLUDING PUBLISHED MUSIC
(Important modern collections and books marked with asterisks)

THE ROBERTSBRIDGE FRAGMENT

Wooldridge, H. E., *Early English Harmony*, Vol. I. Facs., 1897; Vol. II. Transcriptions, 1913.

Wolf, Johannes, 'Zur Geschichte der Orgelmusik im vierzehnten Jahrhundert.' *Kirchenmusikalisches Jahrbuch*, XIV, 1899.*

Handschin, J., 'Über Estampie und Sequenz.' *Zeitschrift für Musikwissenschaft*, 1918 and 1930.

Apel, Willi, *Musik aus früher Zeit* (Schott), Vol. II.

SQUARCIALUPO

Eitner, R., *Monatshefte für Musikgeschichte*, 1885. Article by O. Kade.

THE SAGAN, WINSEM, AND BRESLAU MSS.

Feldmann, F., *Musik und Musikpflege im mittelalterlichen Schlesien*, 1938. (Examples from Sagan MS. and Breslau Qu. 42.)*

Feldmann, F., 'Ein Tabulatur-fragment des Breslauer Dominikaner-Klosters.' *Zeitschrift für Musikwissenschaft*, XV. 1933. (Examples from Breslau, 687a.)*

Schrade, L., 'Die Messe in der Orgel des 15 Jhdts.' *Archiv für Musikforschung*, 1936. (Examples from Winsem MS.)*

Schrade, L., *Die Landschriftliche Überlieferung der ältesten Instrumentaluusik*, 1931. (Also Winsem.)*

Schrade, L., 'The Organ Mass of the Fifteenth Century.' *Musical Quarterly*, (New York), July and Oct., 1942.

THE ILEBORGH TABLATURE

Apel, Willi, 'Die Tablaturen des Adam Ileborgh.' *Zeitschrift für Musikwissenschaft*, 1934.*

CONRAD PAUMANN

Eitner, R., *Monatshefte für Musikgeschichte*. (The Buxheim Organ Book.) Nos. 32, 33 and 34 (1888).

Ameln, Konrad, *Locheimer Liederbuch und Fundamentum Organisandi des C. P.* New Edition in Facsimile, Berlin, 1925.

Arnold, F. W., *Fundamentum Organisandi*, 1926. Revised from Chrysander's Jahrbucher, (1867).*

Apel, W., 'Early German Keyboard Music.' *The Musical Quarterly* (New York), April, 1937. *

Apel, W., *Musik aus früher Zeit*, Vol. I.

THE BUXHEIM ORGAN BOOK

Eitner, R., *Monatshefte für Musikgeschichte*, 1888.*

Schnoor, H., 'Das Buxheimer Orgelbuch.' *Zeitschrift für Musikwissenschaft*, 1921.

PAULUS HOFHAIMER AND HIS SCHOOL

Moser, H J., *Frühmeister der deutschen Orgelbuch*, 1930.*

Moser, H J., *Paulus Hofhaimer, ein Lied- und Orgelmeister des deutschen Humanismus*, 1929.*

Moser, H. J., *Carmina*. Ausgewählte Instrumentalsätze des XVI Jhdts. *Nagels Archiv*, 1929 (instrumental pieces (3, 4 and 5 voices) by Isaac and Senfl, etc.).

Paesler, Carl, 'Das Fundamentbuch von Hans von Konstanz'. (Buchner.) *Vierteljahresschrift für Musikwissenschaft*, 1889.*

Merian, W., 'Die Tabulaturen des Organisten.' (Hans Kotter.) *Sammelbände der Inter. Musikwissenschaft*, 1916.

Gombosi, O., 'Miszellen. Hofhaimeriana.' *Zeitschrift für Musikwissenschaft*, Dec., 1932.

Apel, W., 'Early German Keyboard Music.' *The Musical Quarterly* (New York), April, 1937.*

Webern, A., *Denkmäler der Tonkunst in Österreich*, XVI, i. (Keyboard and Instrumental pieces by Isaac.) Also J. Wolf, XIV, i.*

See also for above works, Apel (Willi), *The Notation of Polyphonic Music* (Mediaeval Academy of America), Cambridge, Mass., 2nd Edition, 1944.*

JOHN REDFORD AND EARLY ENGLISH

Pfatteicher, C. F., *John Redford*, 1934.*

Glyn, Margaret, *Early English Organ Music* (Assoc. Music Press).*

ARNOLT SCHLICK

Eitner, Robert, *Monatshefte für Musikgeschichte*, 1869.

Tapper, W., *Sang und Klang aus Alter Zeit*, 1906.

Bellermann, H. and L., *Die Mensuralnoten und Taktzeichen des XV and XVI Jhdt.* 1906. 4-part setting of *Isaac*, by Schlick.

Harms, Gottlieb, *Tablaturen uff etlicher Lobgesang und Lidlein uff die Orgeln und Lauten.* (Klecken), 1924.*

Kendall, Raymond, 'Notes on Arnolt Schlick.' *Acta Musicologica*, XI, 1939.

See also modern versions by Ernst Flade (Mainz) 1932, and Paul Smets, 1937.

LEONHARD KLEBER

Eitner, Robert, following the '*Buxheimer Orgelbuch.*' *Monatshefte für Musikgeschichte*, 1888.

Lowenfeld, H., *Leonhard Kleber und sein Tablaturbücher*, 1897.

EARLY FRENCH

Rokseth, Y., *Treize Motets et un Prélude pour Orgue.* (Attaignant, 1531.) (Paris) 1930.* Also, *Deux livres d'orgue.* (Attaignant, 1531.) 1925.*

Apel, W., *Musik aus früher Zeit*, Vol. II.

ADRIAN WILLAERT

Eitner, R., *Monatshefte für Musikgeschichte*, XIX.

Hertzmann, E., *A. Willaert*, 1931.

Lenaerts, R., 'Notes sur Adrian Willaert.' (*Extrait Bulletin d'Institut Hist. Belge de Rome.* (Brussels), 1935.

Vocal

Averkamp, A., *Missa super Benedicta. Vereeniging voor Noord-Nederlands Muziek-geschiedenis*, XXXV, (1869) and 1915.

Latham, M., *Dialogo a sette voci. Bach Choir Magazine*, 1892.

Collins, H. B., *Regina Coeli*. Motet. Lond., 1917.

Collins, H. B., *Pater Noster*. Motet. *Polyphonic Motets, No.* 38, 1931.

Zenck, H., *A. Willaert. Sämtliche Werke*, 1937. *Denkmäler Deutscher Tonkunst. Publikationen alter Musik*. Year 9.*

Instrumental

Wasielewski, J. W., *Geschichte der Instrumentalmusik*, 1878.

Tagliapietra, Gino, *Anthology of Ancient and Modern Music for the Pianoforte*, Vol. 1, 1931. (Written as keyboard pieces.)*

Zenck, H., *Neun Ricercari für drei beliebige Instrumente. Antiqua Series, No.* 2316 (Schott) 1933.*

JACHET BUUS

Sutherland, Gordon, 'The Ricercari of Jacques Buus.' *Musical Quarterly*, (New York), Oct., 1945.

GIROLAMO CAVAZZONI

Benvenuti, G., *Cavazzoni. Raccolta Nazionale delle Musiche Italiane*, Nos. 23–27, Milan, 1919.*

Torchi, L., *L'Arte Musicale in Italia*, Vol. III, 1898.*

Tagliapietra, G., *Anthology, etc.*, Vol. I, 1931.*

ANTONIO CABEZÓN AND EARLY SPANISH

Pedrell, F., *Hispaniae schola musica sacra*, Vols. III, IV, VII and VIII, 1894.*

Pedrell, F., *Antología de Organistos Clásicos Españoles*, Madrid, 1908.

Tagliapietra, G., *Anthology, etc.*, Vol. I, 1931.*

Apel, Willi, 'Early Spanish Music for Lute and Keyboard Instruments.' *Musical Quarterly*, (New York), July, 1934. Also Oct., 1938.

Chase, Gilbert, *Music in Spain*, (Dent) 1941.*

ANDREA GABRIELI

Benvenuti, G., *Andrea e G. Gabrieli e la musica strumentale in San Marco*. Preface by G. Cesari. Vol. I, 1931–32.*

Instrumental

Wasielewski, J. W., *Geschichte der Instrumentalmusik*, 1879.

Concina, Giovanni, *Concerti. Libro Primo e Secundo. Dialogo a 8 voci.* (Venice), 1898.

Guilmant, A., and Pirro, A., *Archives des Maîtres de l'Orgue. Liber Fratrum Cruciferorum* (Schott), 1914.

Torchi, L., *L'Arte Musicale in Italia*, Vol. III.*

Tagliapietra, G., *Anthology, etc.*, Vol. I, 1931.*

Vocal

Niedermēyer, L., *Te Deum Patrem ingenitum. La Maîtrise.* 3e Année, No. 11, 1859.

Griesbacher, P., *Missa Brevis* (Coppenrath), 1904.

Killing, J., *Psalm 66. Deus miseratur nostri.* (12 voices). *Kirchenmusikalische Schätze.* Beilage Nr. 5 (Schwann), 1911.

Collins, H. B., *Filiae Jerusalem.* Motet for 4 voices (S. Blyth), 1921.

Norton, H. R., *Missa Brevis* (Frith Press), 1923.

Terry, R. R., *Ecclesiasticorum Cantionum* .Motet. *Polyphonic Motets,* No. 28, 1931.

Einstein, A., *Denkmäler der Tonkunst in Österreich* (Madrigals), XLI, Band 77, 1934. Also : *Angeli archangeli* and *Filiae Jerusalem.* (*Schola Cantorum*); *Sacerdos et Pontifex* and *Coro dolce ben mio* (Madrigal) (Hansen) ; and *Crucifixus* (3 parts) (Augener), (No. 9169 f).

ANNIBALE PADOVANO

Pierront, N., and Hennebains, J. P., *13 Ricercari* (350 limited copies), (Lyre Press), Paris.

Tagliapietra, G., *Anthology,* etc., Vol. I, 1931.

Paz, Valle de, *Annibale Padovano,* 1933.

CLAUDIO MERULO

Catelani, A., *Memorie della vita di Claudio Merulo* (Parma), 1859.

Bigi, Quiro, *De Claudio Merulo da Correggio,* 1861 (with portrait).

Molmenti, P., *La Musica in Venezia a tempo di C. Merulo,* 1904.

Labat, J. B., *Livre des Œuvres d'Orgue,* (Claude Merulo), (Richault), (Paris), 1865.

Kinkeldey, O., *Orgel und Klavier, in der Musik des 16 Jahrhunderts,* 1910.

Guilmant, A., and Pirro, A., *Archives des Maîtres de l'Orgue. Liber Fratrum Cruciferorum* (Schott), 1914.

Torchi, L., *L'Arte Musicale in Italia,* Vol. III.*

Tagliapietra, G., *Anthology, etc.,* Vol. II, 1931.*

GIOVANNI GABRIELI

Winterfeld, J., *Gabrieli und sein Zeitalter,* 1834 (with vocal and instrumental music).

Benvenuti, G., *Andrea e G. Gabrieli e la musica strumentale in San Marco,* Vol. II,* 1931–32.

Bedbrook, G. S. *The Genius of Giovanni Gabrieli* (1557-1612), *The Music Review,* May, 1947.

Instrumental

Reimann, H., *Old Chamber Music* (Sonata a 3 Violini, Canzone a 8), (Augener), (Tempo changes incorrect), (also in a Bärenreiter edition).

Wasielewski, J. W., *Instrumentalsätze vom Ende des XVI bis Ende des XVII Jahrhundert,* 1874.

Einstein, A., *Canzoni per sonar a quattro. Antiqua Series,* No. 2306, (Schott), 1933.

Organ and Keyboard

Wasielewski, J. W., *Geschichte der Instrumentalmusik,* 1878.

Torchi, L., *L'Arte Musicale in Italia,* Vol. III (1898–1907).*

Foschini, G. F., *Antologia Classica Italiana per Organo,* X. *Composizioni per Organo,* 1901. (Ricercare a 3 Soggetti.)

Kinkeldey, O., *Orgel und Klavier, etc.*, 1910.
Tagliapietra, G., *Anthology, etc.*, Vol. II, 1931.*

Choral and Vocal Works

Damrosch, F., *Beata es Virgo Maria* (Schirmer), New York, 1899.
Damrosch, F., *Benedictus.* (Triple Chorus) (Schirmer), New York, 1902.
Damrosch, F., *Jubilate Deo.* (Double Chorus) (Schirmer), New York, 1902.
Damrosch, F., *In ecclesis.* Double Chorus and Organ (Schirmer), 1904. (Not complete with regard to instruments.)
Damrosch, F., *Magnificat for 8 voices. Bach Choir Magazine*, No. 7.
Damrosch, F., *Beata es Virgo Maria.* 6-part Motet. *Bach Choir Magazine*, No. 21B. (1877–98).
Reynolds, G., *Alma cortes'e bella.* (Madrigal.) (J. Fisher & Bro.), Birmingham. New York, 1924.
Williamson, J. F., *Benedixisti.* (7-part.) (Schirmer), 1932.

JAN PIETERSZOON SWEELINCK

Tiedeman, F. H. J., 'J. P. Sweelinck een bio-bibliografische Schets.' (*Vereeniging voor Noord Muziekgeschiedenis*), 1869.
Seiffert, Max, *J. P. Sweelinck und seine direkten deutschen Schuler* (Breitkopf & Härtel), 1891.
Sollitt, E. R., *Dufay to Sweelinck* (Washburn), 1933.
Meyer, B. Van den Sigtenhorst, *Jan P. Sweelinck en zijn instrumentale musiek* (Alsbach), 1934.
Seiffert, Max, *Werken . . . uitgegeven door de Vereeniging voor Noord-Nederlands Muziekgeschiedenis. Werken voor Orgel of Klavier,* Vol. 1. Also Vol. IX. Vol. X, a reprint of his work on composition. (Vocal works in remaining Vols.) (Breitkopf & Härtel), (Alsbach). Also reprint of works : *Werken voor Orgel en Clavecimbel van Jan Pieterszoon Sweelinck.* (Alsbach), 1943.*

Keyboard Music

West, J. E., *Fantasia cromatica* (Novello), 1909.
Tagliapietra, G., *Anthology, etc.*, Vol. III, 1932.*
Doflein, E., *Ludvariationen für Klavier* (3 *Variations for Cembalo or Organ*) (Schott), 1935.
Meyer, B. Van den Sigtenhorst, *Werken van Jan P. Sweelinck.*
  1. *Toccata* (3rd tone).
  2. *Kleine Toccata.*
  3. *Variaties over 'Est-ce-Mars'.*
  4. *Fantasie op de manier van een echo.*
  5. *Chromatische Fantasie* (2nd Tone).
  7. *Hexachord—Fantasie.*
  8. *Variaties over 'Ich voer al over rhijn'.*

Choral and Vocal Works

Meyer, Van den Sigtenhorst, *Werken van Jan. P. Sweelinck*, No. 6. *Yeux, qui guidez mon âme* (Terzet).
Vereeniging voor Nederlandsche Musiekgeschiedenis.
  1. *Regina Coeli* (5 part).

2. *8 Psalms* (6 part).
7. *Bouch de Coral* (2 part).
15. *Hodie Christus natus est.*
18. *Psalm* 150 (8 part).

HANS LEO HASSLER

Zolle, G. F., *Lustgarten. Gesellschaft für Musikforschung.* Bd. XV, 1887.
Werra, E von, *Hans Leo Hassler. Werke.* Vol. I. *Werken für Orgel und Klavier, Denkmäler Deutscher Tonkunst.* 2nd series, 1903.*

ENGLISH VIRGINAL COMPOSERS

Naylor, E. W., *An Elizabethan Virginal Book* (Dent, 1905).
Borren, Van den, *The Sources of Keyboard Music in England* (Curwen), 1912.
Anderton, H. O., *Early English Music* (*Musical Opinion Publication*), 1920.
Hadow, Sir W. H., *William Byrd* (Oxf. Univ. Press), 1923.
Glyn, Margaret, *About Elizabethan Virginal Music and its Composers* (Reeves), 1926.
Howes, Frank S., *William Byrd* (K. Paul), 1928.
Fellowes, E. H., *William Byrd* (Oxf. Univ. Press), 1948.*
Fellowes, E. H., *Orlando Gibbons* (Oxf. Univ. Press), 1925.*
Henry, Leigh, *Dr. John Bull* (Herbert Joseph), 1937.
Miller, Hugh M., 'John Bull's Organ Works.' *Music and Letters,* Jan., 1947.

COLLECTIONS OF KEYBOARD MUSIC

Fuller-Maitland, J. A., and Squire, W. Barclay, *The Fitzwilliam Virginal Book* (Breitkopf & Härtel), 1894.*
Fuller-Maitland, J. A., *Twenty-Five Pieces for Keyed Instruments* (Cosyn's Book), (Chester), 1923.
Andrews, Hilda, *My Ladye Nevell's Booke* (Curwen), 1926.*
Glyn, Margaret, *Thirty Virginal Pieces* (Stainer & Bell), 1927.
Glyn, Margaret, *Parthenia* (Reeves), 1927. Also Tagliapietra. *Anthology, etc.,* Vols. II and III; Apel, W., *Musik aus früher Zeit,* Vol. II and other collections.*

WILLIAM BYRD (MUSIC)

Bantock, Sir Granville, *Three Dances* (Novello), 1912.
Bantock, Sir Granville, *Album of Selected Pieces* (Novello), 1913.
Fuller-Maitland, J. A., and Squire, W. Barclay, *Fourteen Pieces for Keyed Instruments* (Stainer & Bell), 1923.
Fuller-Maitland, J. A., and Squire, W. Barclay, *Fitzwilliam Virginal Book. Selected Pieces,* Vol. I (British Continental).
Glyn, Margaret, *The Byrd Organ Book* (Reeves), 2 Vols., 1923.*
Glyn, Margaret, *Dances Grave and Gay* (Rogers), 1923.
Glyn, Margaret, *Pavans and Galliards* (Assoc. Music Press).
Glyn, Margaret, *Selections of Keyboard Pieces* (Fitzwilliam Book), 2 Vols. (British Continental), 1944–45.
Farnam, G. L., *Miserere* (from Fitzwilliam Book), (Gray, New York), 1927.

GILES FARNABY

Bantock, Sir Granville, *Album of Selected Pieces* (Novello), 1912.
Fuller-Maitland, J. A., and Squire, W. Barclay, *Fitzwilliam Virginal Book. Selected Pieces,* Vol. II (British Continental).
Glyn, Margaret, *Selections of Keyboard Pieces.* (Fitzwilliam Book), (British Continental), 2 Vols., 1927.
Fellowes, Edmund H., For Two Virginals (Fitzwilliam Book), (2 Piano Series, No. 1a.) (Oxf. Univ. Press), 1934.
   See also Gratton-Flood, W. H., 'Farnaby' (*Musical Times*), July, 1926.

DR. JOHN BULL

Bantock, Sir Granville, *Album of Selected Pieces* (Novello), 1912.
Fuller-Maitland, J. A., and Squire, W. Barclay, *Fitzwilliam Virginal Book. Selected Pieces,* Vol. II (British Continental).
West, J. E., *Two Pieces:*—'*Vexilla regis prodeunt*', Fantasia on Flemish Chorale '*Laet ons net herten reijne*'. (*Old English Organ Music*, No. 25), 1906.
Glyn, Margaret, *John Bull* (J. Williams), 1922.
Glyn, Margaret, *John Bull*, 2 Vols. (Stainer & Bell), 1928. (From the series *Elizabethan Virginal Composers.*)
Glyn, Margaret, *Selections of Keyboard Pieces,* 2 Vols., (Fitzwilliam Book) (British Continental), 1927.

THOMAS WEELKES

Glyn, Margaret, *Pieces for Keyed Instruments* (Stainer & Bell), 1924.

ORLANDO GIBBONS

Glyn, Margaret, *Orlando Gibbons* (J. Williams), 1922 (Elizabethan Virginal Composers).
Glyn, Margaret, *Orlando Gibbons. Complete Works.* 5 Vols. (Vols. 4 and 5 Organ.) (Stainer & Bell), 1925.*

INSTRUMENTAL

Byrd

Fellowes, E. H., *Fantazia for String Sextet or Small Stringed Orchestra* (From *Psalms, Songs and Sonnets, 1611*) (Stainer & Bell), 1922.
Fellowes, E. H., *Fantazia (No. 2) for String Sextet (etc.)* (Stainer & Bell), 1922.
Fellowes, E. H., *Pavan and Galliard for Strings* (Stainer & Bell), 1931.

Gibbons

Fellowes, E. H., *Nine Fantasias for Strings in three parts* (Stainer & Bell), 1924.
Fellowes, E. H., *Fantazia for Stringed Quartet or Small Stringed Orchestra* (Stainer & Bell), 1925.
Meyer, E. H., *Three Part Fantasias (à 3),* (Baerenreiter).
   Also: Terry, Sir R. R., *In Nomines (Two) of Robert Parsons & Parsley* (London), 1923; Fellowes, E. H., *Fantasia a 6* (by Thomas Tomkins) (Stainer & Bell); and *Elizabethan Dance Tunes* (Eight) (Stainer & Bell).

For vocal works of Byrd see Fellowes, *The Collected Works of William Byrd* (Stainer & Bell), 16 Vols. (1937-   ).

Consult also *Grove's Dictionary and Supplement* under 'Virginal Music' for accounts of the English manuscript books. Also Gerald Cooper's article on 'Instrumental Music' in *Oxf. Hist. of Music, Vol.* 2 (2nd Edition), 1927. Davey (H.) *History of English Music,* 1921.

FRESCOBALDI

Haberl, F. X., *Kirchenmusikalisches Jahrbuch,* 1887. *Collectio Musices Organicae* (Breitkopf & Härtel), 1889.*

Bennabi, N., *Ferrara a Girolamo Frescobaldi nel terzo centenario,* 1908.

Ronga, L., *Frescobaldi* (Torino), 1930.*

Keyboard

Pauer, E., *Alter Meister* Series, Bd. IV. 6 *Toccatas for Klavier,* 1882.

Chilesotti, O., *Toccate e Partite d'Intavolatura di Cembalo* (Ricordi), 1910.

West, J. E., *Capriccio sopra La, Sol, Fa, Mi, Re, Ut* (Novello), 1906.

West, J. E., *Capriccio on the notes of the Cuckoo* (Novello), 1907.

West, J. E., *Ricercare in the Dorian Mode* (Novello), 1909.

West, J. E., *Canzone in G Minor* (Novello), 1906.

Casella, A., *Composizioni per Organo e Cembalo,* 1916. (*Raccolta Naz. delle Mus. Ital. Quad.,* 43–47.)

Bogen, F., 16 *Ricercari* (Ricordi and Nationale Edition, Paris), 1918.*

Bogen, F., 25 *Canzoni per Cembalo ed Organo* (Ricordi and Nationale Edition, Paris), 1922.*

Bogen, F., *Partite per Clavicembalo* (Ricordi and Nationale Edition, Paris), 1922.*

Bogen, F., *Correnti per Clavicembalo* (Ricordi and Nationale Edition, Paris), 1922.*

Bonnet, J., and Guilmant, M. A., *Fiori Musicali pour Orgue.* (*Les Grands Maîtres Anciens de l'Orgue*) (Paris), 1922.

Tagliapietra G., *Anthology, etc.,* Vols. IV and V, 1931.*

Harwood, B., *Fugue in A Minor* (Oxf. Univ. Press), 1935.[1]

Bourne, T. W., *Three Fugues for the Organ* (J. B. Cramer), 1937.[1]

Germani (Fernando), *Toccate e Partite.* Parts I and II (de Santis) Rome, 1936–37.*

Instrumental and Vocal

Bogen, F., and Bonaventura, A., *Primo Libro d'Arie Musicali* (Songs), 1933.

David, H., *Canzoni a due Canti. 5 Instrumental Canzoni. Antiqua Series No.* 2304 (Schott), 1933.

SAMUEL SCHEIDT

Seiffert, Max, *Tablatura Nova. Denkmäler Deutscher Tonkunst.* 1st Series. Vol.1, 1892.*

Harms, Gottlieb, *Samuel Scheidt. Werken.* (Klecken), 1923.

[1] Taken from Clementi's Practical Harmony (c. 1810). The style is much later and it is doubtful if they are Frescobaldi's works.

ITALY. (RENAISSANCE GENERALLY)

Straeten, Van der, *Les Musiciens Néerlandais en Italie* (Brussels), 1882.
Dent, E. J., 'Music of the Renaissance.' (*Annual Italian Lecture*), *Proceedings of the British Acad*. Vol. XIX.*
Robeck, N. de, *Music of the Italian Renaissance* (Medici Press), 1928.*
Prunières, H., *A New History of Music* (English Trans.), 1942.*
Lang, P. H., *Music in Western Civilization*, 1942.*

THE VENETIAN SCHOOL

Caffi, F., *Storia della musica sacra di San Marco in Venezia*. 2 Vols., 1854. (Also French translation).
Naumann, E., 'Das goldene Zeitalter der Tonkunst in Venedig,' 1866. (In Virchow's *Sammlung Gemeinverständlicher Wissenschaftlicher Vörtrage*).
Solenti, A., *Rivista Musicale Italiana*, 1902. ('Le rappresentazioni musicali di Venezia dal 1571–1605') (Early stage 'representations' with music).
Molmenti, G., *The Renaissance in Venice*, 1907.
Tebassini, G., 'L'anima musicale di Venezia', *Rivista Musicale Italiana*, 1908.
Borren, Van den, *Les Débuts de la musique à Venise*, 1914.
   See Benvenuti, G., under G. Gabrieli.

EARLY ORGANS AND ORGAN MUSIC, AND OTHER KEYED INSTRUMENTS

Hill, A. G., *Organ Cases and Organs of the Middle Ages and Renaissance*. 2 Vols. 1883–92.
Hill, A. G., *The English Medieval Church Organ*, 1888.
Williams, Abdy C. F., *The Story of the Organ;* and *The Story of Organ Music*. (*Music Story Series*), 1905.
Schering, A., 'Die Niederländische Orgelmesse im Zeitalter des Josquin.' (*Studien zur Musikgeschichte*), 1912.
Pirro, A., *Les Clavecinistes*, 1926.
Raugel, F., *Les Organistes*, 1923.
Cooper, Gerald, Article in *Oxf. Hist. of Music*. Vol. II (2nd Edit.), 1929.*
James, P., *Early Keyboard Instruments* (London), 1930.*
Mueren, F. van der, *Het Orgel in der Nederlanden* (Leuven), 1931.
Le Cerf et Labande (Arnault de Zwolle), *Instruments de musique du XVe siècle*. 1932.
Klotz, H., *Über die Orgelmusik der Gotik, der Renaissance, und der Barock* (Kassel), 1934.*
Dufourcq, Norbert, *Esquisse d'une histoire de l'orgue en France* (Paris), 1935.*
Hickman, Hans, *Das Portative* (Kassel), 1936.
Frotscher, G., *Geschichte des Orgelspiels und der Orgelkomposition*, 1933–36. (Largest complete work).*
Apel, W., 'Early German Keyboard Music.' *The Musical Quarterly* (New York), 1937.*
See p. 214 of Dufourcq's work for list of articles, etc., on the organs of different countries.

Early Keyboard Dance Music

Merian, W., 'Der Tanz in den deutschen Tabulaturbüchern' (*Samml. der Inter. Musikgesellschaft*), 1927.

Halbig, Hermann, *Klaviertänze des XVII Jhdts.*

Collections of Early Keyboard Music
(To early 17th Century)

Ritter, G. G., *Geschichte des Orgelspiels.* 2 Vols., 1884.

Tagliapietra, G., *Anthology of Ancient and Modern Music for the Pianoforte.* Vols. I–VI. . . .*

Apel, W., *Musik aus früher Zeit.* 2 Vols. (Schott).*

Torchi, L., *L'Arte Musicale in Italia.* Vols. III and IV.*

Davison, A. T., and Apel, W., *Historical Anthology of Music* (Oxf. Univ. Press), 1947.*

RECORDED MUSIC

Records marked with a 'star' have items on the other side. With the exception of titles in brackets the original names on the records have been retained.

1. 14th and 15th Centuries	English Dance (c. 1350) Coloured Song (Paumann) (Evolution of the Keyboard Series)	Sylvia Marlowe (Harpsichord)	Bost. 104★
2. Landini	Questa Fanciulla (Pathé Organ Records)	André Marchal (Organ)	Pathé Pat. 63★
3. Landini	Benche ora piova (Early Organ Music Series)	Carl Weinrich (Organ)	Musicraft 1047 Set 9★
4. Ivrea MS.	El Molin de Paris. 14th century	Joseph Bonnet	Victor 18413
5. Paumann	Benedicite Allmechtger Got Her Jesu Cris (Lochei-mer Liederbuch No. 74)	Yves Tinayre (Tenor) (Organ accompaniment)	Lumen 32012
6. Hofhaimer	Fantasia on 'On freudt verzer'	Carl Weinrich (Organ)	Musicraft 1047 Set 9. (See 3)
7. Attaignant F. Bendusi	French Basse Dance (1530) Dance (1553)	Sylvia Marlowe (Harpsichord)	Bost. 104 (See 1)
8. Cabezón	Diferencias sobre 'El Canto de Caballero'	Carl Weinrich (Organ)	Musicraft 1048
9. Cabezón	Diferencias sobre 'El Canto de Caballero'	Joseph Bonnet (Organ)	Anthologie Sonore 69★
10. Cabezón	Tiento (on 1st Tone)	André Marchal (Organ)	Pathé Pat. 65★
11. Cabezón	Tiento (on 1st Tone)	Finn Viderö (Organ)	H.M.V. DA 5207
12. Tomas de Santa Maria	Fantasia (on the 3rd tone)	Finn Viderö (Organ)	H.M.V. DA 5207
13. Tomas de Santa Maria	Clausula de Octavo tono; Tiento (Cabanillos) (1644 –1712)	Joseph Bonnet (Organ)	Anthologie Sonore 69 (See 9)
14. Tomas de Santa Maria	Harmonisation of Melody (?) Passacaglia in D Minor (Cabanillos)	André Marchal (Organ)	Pathé Pat. 65 (See 10)

No.	Composer	Work	Performer	Recording
15.	B. Schmid	Passamezzo (Ungaro Saltarello Suo)	Ernst Victor Wolff (Harpsichord)	American Columbia 69328 D.*
16.	B. Schmid	Gagliarde	Alfred Sittard (Organ)	Polydor. 95157. Decca CA 8149. Brunswick 90033
17.	Ammerbach	Passamezzo	Sylvia Marlowe (Harpsichord)	Bost. 104. (See 1, 7 and 26)
18.	Andrea Gabrieli	Canzona in F (Canzoni alla francese); Ricercar (Palestrina) (Pathé Organ Records)	Charles Hens (Organ)	Pathé Pat. 63 (See 2)
19.	Andrea Gabrieli	Pass' e mezo antico in (cinque) modi variati	Anna Linde (Harpsichord)	Musica Italiana Antiqua 5
20.	Andrea Gabrieli	Instrumental. (a) Three Ricercari (on the 6th, 2nd and 12th tone)	Stuyvesant Quartet	American Columbia 703660
21.	Giovanni Gabrieli	Ricercar on the 10th tone	Marcel Dupré (Organ)	Anthologie Sonore 4*
22a.	Giovanni Gabrieli	Instrumental (a) Sonata pian e forte	Cornets, Trombones and Altos	Anthologie Sonore 25a
22b.	Giovanni Gabrieli	(b) Canzon a six (Canzoni et Sonate) (1615)	Cornets, Trombones and Altos	Anthologie Sonore 25b
23.	Giovanni Gabrieli	Processional and Ceremonial Music: In ecclesis; O Jesu mi dulcissime; Jubilate Deo	Voices, Organ and Brass. Boston Symphony Orchestra. Harvard Glee Club. Radcliffe Choral Soc., etc.	Victor (4) D.A. Set 928
24.	Sweelinck	Ekko Fantasia (No. 11) (Echo) (Early Organ Music)	Carl Weinrich (Organ)	Musicraft 1049*
25.	Sweelinck	Fantasia (Echo) (No. 10)	Finn Viderö (Organ)	H.M.V. DB 5214*
26.	G. M. Trabacci	Ricercata (Evolution of the Keyboard Series)	Sylvia Marlowe (Harpsichord)	Bost. 104. (See 1, 7 and 17)
27.	Titelouze	Ave Maria Stella (Early Organ Music)	Carl Weinrich (Organ)	Musicraft 1049 (See 24)

28. Byrd	The Bells (Fitzwilliam Book. No. 69)	Pauline Aubert (Virginal)	Anthologie Sonore 14*
29. Byrd	The Bells (Fitzwilliam Book. No. 69)	Ernst Victor Wolf (Harpsichord)	American Columbia 69328 D (See 15)
30. Byrd	The Bells (Fitzwilliam Book. No. 69)	Alice Ehlers	Homochord 4-8760
31. Byrd	Pavan and Galliard (Earl of Salisbury)	R. Dolmetsch (Virginal)	Columbia 5712 (Also on Dolmetsch Record DR. 4)
32. Byrd	Pavan (Earl of Salisbury)	Alice Ehlers (Harpsichord)	Decca F 7726*
33. Byrd	Variations on 'O Mistresse Mine' (Fitz. Book No. 66)	George Dyson (Pianoforte)	Columbia D 40137
34. Byrd	Wolsey's Wilde (Fitz. Book No. 157)	Wanda Landowska	H.M.V. DA 1014 Victor 1599
35a. Byrd	Earle of Oxford's Marche; (Fitz. Book No. 259) Queen's Alaman (Fitz. Book No. 171) Galliard (Fitz. Book No. 255)	Violet Gordon Woodhouse (Harpsichord)	H.M.V. E 294
35b. Byrd	Rowland (Fitz. Book No. 160)		H.M.V. E 295
36. Byrd	Sellinger's Round (Fitz. Book No. 64)	Edwin Bodky (Harpsichord)	American Decca 20163 Parlophone German B.3.7029 English R.1023
37. Byrd	Miserere (Fitz. Book No. 176)	Carl Weinrich (Organ)	Musicraft 1048
38. Byrd	Galliard: (MS. Drexel. N.Y.) Lulla	Isabelle Nef (Harpsichord)	L'Oiseau Lyre 76
39. Farnaby	His Toye; His Dreame; His Rest (Columbia History of Music Vol. 1) Also Bull's King's Hunt (Fitz. Book Nos. 260, 195, 270)	R. Dolmetsch (Virginal)	Columbia C 5713

No.	Composer	Title	Performer	Recording
40.	Farnaby.	Rosa Solis (Fitz. Book No. 143)	Ernst Victor Wolff (Harpsichord)	American Columbia 69328 D. (See 15)
41.	Farnaby	His Humour (Fitz. Book No. 196) (Inter. Educ. Soc)	George Dyson (Pianoforte)	Columbia D 40139*
42.	Farnaby	The New Sa-Hoo (Fitz. Book No. 148)	Pauline Aubert (Virginal)	Anthologie Sonore 14. (See 28)
43.	Farnaby	Tower Hill (Fitz. Book No. 245)	L. Richards (Harpsichord)	Brunswick B 3206
44.	Dr. John Bull	Gigge (Dr. Bull's Myselfe) (Fitz. Book No. 189)	Anna Linde (Harpsichord)	Parlophone: German P. 9005, English 10524, American Decca 25036
45.	Dr. John Bull	Gigge (Dr. Bull's Myselfe) (Inter. Educ. Soc.)	George Dyson (Harpsichord)	Columbia D 40139. (See 41 and 47)
46.	Dr. John Bull	Galliard	Violet Gordon Woodhouse (Harpsichord)	H.M.V. E 275
47.	Dr. John Bull (See also 39)	King's Hunt (Fitz. Book No. 135)	George Dyson	Columbia D 40139 (See 41 and 45)
48.		Jig (Bull) A Toye (Farnaby) Galliard (Peter Philips) etc. (Evolution of the Keyboard Series)	Sylvia Marlowe (Harpsichord)	Bost. 105*
49.	P. Philips	Galliard (Early Keyboard Music)	George Dyson (Harpsichord)	Columbia D 40138
50.	O. Gibbons	The Lord Salisbury, His Pavan; The Queen's Command	Ralph Kirkpatrick	Musicraft 1087
51.	Frescobaldi	Fugue in G. Minor	W. Fisher (Organ)	Polydor 65758
52.	Frescobaldi	Toccata for the Elevation	Marcel Dupré (Organ)	Anthologie Sonore No. 4. (See 21)
53.	Frescobaldi	Toccata for the Elevation	Joseph Bonnet (Organ)	Pathé Pat. 64

159

54. Frescobaldi	Toccata for the Elevation	Prof. Vignanelli (Organ)	Musique au Vatican V 1141 (S.E.M.S.) (See 57)
55. Frescobaldi	Toccata IX (Libro II); Caprice Pastorale (From Toccatas 1637)	Fernando Germani	Musique au Vatican V. 1179 (S.E.M.S.) Bost. 105 (See 48)
56. Frescobaldi	La Frescobaldi (Aria detta la Frescobalda) (With Toccata No. 2 of Froberger)	Sylvia Marlowe (Harpsichord)	
57. Frescobaldi	La Frescobaldi (Aria detta la Frescobalda)	Prof. Vignanelli (Organ)	Musique au Vatican (S.E.M.S.) V. 1141 (See 54)
58. Frescobaldi	La Frescobaldi (Aria detta la Frescobalda) and Quattuor Galiarde	Anna Linde (Harpsichord)	Musica Italiana Antiqua No. 6
59. Frescobaldi	Toccata sopra i pedali	Finn Viderö (Organ)	H.M.V. DB 5214 (See 25)
60. Frescobaldi	Galliard	Alice Ehlers (Harpsichord)	Decca F 7726 (See 32)
61. S. Scheidt	Chorale Paraphrase 'Credo'	Marcel Dupré (Organ)	Anthologie Sonore 10
62. S. Scheidt	Vom Himmel hoch; Puer Natus; O Jesulein Süss.	Yella Pessel (Harpsichord)	American Columbia 17071 D
63. S. Scheidt	Choral-Prelude on 'Herzlich tut mich Verlangen'	E. Weiss-Mann (Harpsichord)	Mary Howard Set
64. S. Scheidt	Var on Chorale: Da Jesus dem Kreuze stund	Finn Viderö	H.M.V. DB 5213
65. Christian Erbach (1570–1635)	Canzona in G	Alfred Sittard (Organ)	Polydor 10257 Decca PO 5110

ADDENDA

William Byrd	Keyboard Pieces (unnamed)	Hélène Pignari (Pianoforte)	L'Oiseau-Lyre 88–89

NEW BIBLIOGRAPHY
Edited by Frederick Freedman

A. *Recent Literature on Early Keyboard Music*
Compiled by G. S. Bedbrook
14th & 15th Century Keyboard Music

Italian

Fischer, Kurt von. "The MS Paris, Bibliothèque Nationale, Nouvelle Acquisition Française 6771," *Musica Disciplina* XI (1957), 38–78.

Göllner, Theodor. "Landinis 'Questa fanciulla' bei Oswald von Wolkenstein," *Die Musikforschung* XVII/4 (October–December 1964), 393–98.

Pirrotta, Nino. "Note su un codice di antiche musiche per tastiera [Faenza 117]," *Rivista Musicale Italiana* LVI/4 (October–December 1954), 333–9.

Plamenac, Dragan. "Keyboard Music of the 14th Century in Codex Faenza 117," *Journal of the American Musicological Society* IV/3 (Fall 1951), 179–201.

————. "A note on the Rearrangement of Faenza Codex 117," *Journal of the American Musicological Society* XVII/1 (Spring 1964), 78–81.

————. "New Light on Codex Faenza 117," in: *Kongressbericht, Internationale Gesellschaft für Musikwissenschaft, 5th Kongress (Utrecht 1952)* (Amsterdam: Alsbach, 1953), 310–26.

German

Bedbrook, Gerald Stares. "The Buxheim Keyboard Manuscript," *The Music Review* XIV/4 (November 1953), 288–95.

Göllner, Theodor von. "Notationsfragmente aus einer Organistenwerkstatt des 15, Jahrhunderts," *Archiv für Musikwissenschaft* XXIV/3 (July 1967), 170–7.

Petzsch, Christoph. "Zu den Autorennamen im Anhang von Konrad Paumanns Fundamentum Organisandi," *Archiv für Musikwissenschaft* XXI/3-4 (1964), 200–11.

Reichling, Alfred. "Ein bisher unbeachteter Kyriesatz nebst zugehörigem Praembulum im Buxheimer Orgelbuch," *Die Musikforschung* IX/4 (1956), 443–6.

Schrammek, Winfried. "Zur Numerierung in Buxheimer Orgelbuch," *Die Musikforschung* IX/3 (1956), 298–302.

Siebert, Frederick Mark. "Mass Sections in the *Buxheim Organ Book:* A Few Points," *The Musical Quarterly* L/3 (July 1964), 353–66.

Southern, Eileen. *The Buxheim Organ Book.* Brooklyn: Institute of Medieval Music, 1962. (*Musicological Studies,* 6).

Others

Dart, Thurston. "A New Source of Early English Organ Music," *Music and Letters* XXXV/3 (July 1954), 201–5.

Southern, Eileen. "Some Keyboard Basse Dances of the Fifteenth Century," *Acta Musicologica* XXXV (1963), 114–24.

Rokseth, Yvonne. *La Musique d'orgue au XVᵉ siècle et au début de XVIᵉ.* Paris: Librairie E. Droz, 1930.

————. "The Instrumental Music of the Middle Ages and Early Sixteenth Century," in: *The New Oxford History of Music* [*Ars Nova and the Renaissance 1300–1540,* Dom Anselm Hughes and Gerald Abraham, eds.]. (London: Oxford University Press, 1960), III, 406–65.

16th Century and Later Keyboard Music
German

Apel, Willi. "Die Celler Orgeltabulatur von 1601," *Die Musikforschung* XIX/2 (April–June 1966), 142–51.

Breig, Werner. "Die Lübbenauer Tabulaturen Lynar A1 und A2; Eine quellenkündliche Studie," *Archiv für Musikwissenschaft* XXV/2 (June 1968), 96–117; XXV/3 (August 1968), 223–36.

Dickinson, A.E.F. "The Lübbenau Keyboard Books; a further Note on Faceless Features," *The Music Review* XXVII/4 (November 1966), 270–86.

Eisenberg, Jacob. "Virdung's Keyboard Illustrations," *Galpin Society Journal* XV (March 1962), 82–8.

Flade, Ernst. "Literarische Zeugnisse zur Empfindung der *Farbe* und *Farbigkeit* bei der Orgel und beim Orgelspiel in Deutschland, ca. 1500–1620," *Acta Musicologica* XXVIII/4 (October-December 1956), 176–206.

Lenneberg, Hans H. "The Critic Criticized: Sebastian Virdung and his Controversy with Arnolt Schlick," *Journal of the American Musicological Society* X/1 (Spring 1956), 1–6.

Reimann, Margarete. "Pasticcios und Parodien in norddeutschen Klaviertabulaturen," *Die Musikforschung* VIII/3 (1955), 265–71.

White, John Reeves. "The Tablature of Johannes of Lublin; MS 1716 of the Polish Academy of Sciences in Cracow," *Musica Disciplina* XVII (1963), 137–62.

Italian

Apel, Willi. "The Early Development of the Organ Ricercar," *Musica Disciplina* III/2–4 (1949), 139–50.

Burns, Joseph A. "Antonio Valente, Neapolitan Keyboard Primitive," *Journal of the American Musicological Society* XII/2–3 (Summer-Fall 1959), 133–43.

Dart, Thurston. "Cavazzoni and Cabezón," *Music and Letters* XXXVI/1 (January 1955), 2–6.

Jeppesen, Knud. "Cavazzoni-Cabezón," *Journal of the American Musicological Society* VIII/2 (Summer 1955), 81–5.

Machabey, Armand. *Gerolamo Frescobaldi Ferraransis* (1583–1643). Paris: La Colombe, 1952.

Slim, H. Colin. "Keyboard Music at Castell'Arquato by an Early Madrigalist," *Journal of the American Musicological Society* XV/1 (Spring 1962), 35–47.

English

Dart, Thurston. "New Sources of Virginal Music," *Music and Letters* XXXV/2 (April 1954), 93–106.

———. "A New Source of Early English Organ Music," *Music and Letters* XXXV/3 (July 1954), 201–5.

Dickinson, A. E. F. "English Virginal Music," *The Music Review* XVI/1 (February 1955), 13–28.

Donington, Robert, and Thurston Dart. "The Origin of the In Nomine," *Music and Letters* XXX/2 (April 1949), 101–6.

Ferguson, Howard. "Repeats and Final Bars in the Fitzwilliam Virginal Book," *Music and Letters* XLIII/4 (October 1962), 345–50.

Lowinsky, Edward E. "English Organ Music of the Renaissance," *The Musical Quarterly* XXXIX/3 (July 1953), 373–95; XXXIX/4 (October 1953), 528–53.

Mellers, Wilfrid. "John Bull and English Keyboard Music," *The Musical Quarterly* XL/3 (July 1954), 364–83: XL/4 (October 1954), 548–71.

Stevens, Denis. "Pre-Reformation Organ-Music in England," *Proceedings of the Royal Musical Association* LXXVIII (1951/2), 1–10.

———. "A Unique Tudor Organ Mass," *Musica Disciplina* VI/4 (1952), 167–75.

———. *The Mulliner Book. A Commentary.* London: Stainer & Bell, 1952.

———. "Thomas Preston's Organ Mass," *Music and Letters* XXXIX/1 (January 1958), 29–34.

Ward, John. "Les sources de la musique pour le clavier en Angleterre," in: Jean Jacquot, ed., *La musique instrumentale de la Renaissance* (Paris: Éditions du Centre Nationale de la Recherche Scientifique, 1955), 225–36.

French

Apel, Willi. "Attaingnant: Quatorze Gaillardes," *Die Musikforschung* XIV/4 (October–December 1961), 361–70.

Dufourcq, Norbert. *La Musique d'Orgue Française de Jehan Titelouze à Jehan Alain, les Artistes et les Oeuvres, les Formes et les Styles,* 2nd ed. Paris: Floury, 1949.

Douglass, Fenner and M. A. Vente. "French Organ Registration in the Early 16th Century," *The Musical Quarterly* LI/4 (October 1965), 614–35.

Spanish

Apel, Willi. "Spanish Organ Music of the Early 17th Century," *Journal of the American Musicological Society* XV/2 (Summer 1962), 174–81.

Howell, Jr., Almonte C. "Cabezón: An Essay in Structural Analysis," *The Musical Quarterly* L/1 (January 1964), 18–30.

Kastner, Santiago. *Antonio de Cabezón.* Coimbra: Coimbra Editora, 1947.

———. "Parallels and Discrepancies between English and Spanish Keyboard Music of the Sixteenth and Seventeenth Century," *Anuario Musical* VII (1952), 77–115.

———. "Rapports entre Schlick et Cabezón," in: Jean Jacquot, ed., *La musique instrumentale de la Renaissance* (Paris: Éditions du Centre Nationale de la Recherche Scientifique, 1955), 217–23.

164

————. "Relations entre la musique instrumentale française et espagnole au XVIᵉ siècle," *Anuario Musical* X (1955), 84–108; XI (1956), 91–110.

General Works on Keyboard Music

Apel, Willi. *Masters of the Keyboard: a Basic Survey of Pianoforte Music.* Cambridge: Harvard University Press, 1947.

————. *The History of Keyboard Music to 1700*, translated and revised by Hans Tischler. Bloomington: Indiana University Press, 1972. (Originally as: *Geschichte der Orgel- und Klaviermusik bis 1700.* Kassel: Bären-reiter, 1967).

Frotscher, Gotthold. *Geschichte des Orgelspiels und der Orgelkomposition,* 2 vols. Berlin–Schöneberg: M. Hesse, 1928–35. Reprint, Berlin: Merseburger, 1959.

Gillespie, Joyn. *Five Centuries of Keyboard Music.* Belmont, Calif.: Wadsworth, 1965.

Horsley, Imogene. "The 16th-Century Variation: A New Historical Survey," *Journal of the American Musicological Society* XII/2–3 (Summer–Fall 1959), 118–32.

————. "The Sixteenth Century Variation and Baroque Counterpoint," *Musica Disciplina* XIV (1960), 159–65.

Kirby, F. E. *A Short History of Keyboard Music.* New York: Free Press, 1966.

Le Huray, Peter. "Early Keyboard Music on the Gramophone," *Music and Letters* XLI/1 (January 1960), 46–52.

Young, William. "Keyboard Music to 1600," *Musica Disciplina* XVI (1962), 115–50; XVII (1963), 163–93.

The Early Organ and Other Keyboard Instruments

Apel, Willi. "The Early History of the Organ," *Speculum* XXIII/2 (April 1948), 191–216.

Boston, J. L. "An Early Virginal-Maker in Chester, and His Tools," *The Galpin Society Journal* VII (April 1954), 3–6.

Clutton, Cecil. "Arnault's MS," *The Galpin Society Journal* V (March 1952), 3–8.

Hubbard, Frank. *Three Centuries of Harpsichord Making.* Cambridge: Harvard University Press, 1963.

Le Cerf, Georges and E.-R. Labande, eds. *Instruments de musique du XVᵉ siècle. Les Traités d'Henri-Arnaut de Zwolle, et de divers anonymes* (MS. B.N. Latin 7295). Paris: A. Picard, 1932.

Nef, Walter. "The Polychord," *The Galpin Society Journal* IV (June 1951), 20–24.

Orth, Siegfried. "Das Wirken des Breslauer Orgelbauers Stephen Kaschendorff in Erfurt (1480–1484)," *Archiv für Musikwissenschaft* XXV/2 (June 1968), 148–50.

Russel, Raymond. *The Harpsichord and Clavichord: An Introductory Study.* London: Faber & Faber, 1959.

Sartori, Claudio. "Organs, Organ-Builders, and Organists in Milan, 1450–1476: New and Unpublished Documents," *The Musical Quarterly* XLIII/1 (January 1957), 57–67.

16th Century Organs and Organ Building

Blanton, J. Edwin. *The Revival of the Organ Case.* Alban, Texas: Venture Press, 1965.

Dufourcq, Norbert. "Recent Researches into French Organ-Building from the Fifteenth to the Seventeenth Century," *The Galpin Society Journal* X (May 1957), 66–81.

Schlick, Arnolt. *Spiegel der Orgelmacher und Organisten,...* Reprint, Mainz: Der Rheingold Verlag, 1932.

Haacke, Walter. *Organs of the World,* Eng. trans. by Marcus Wells. London: Allen & Uuwin, 1966.

Lunelli, Renato. *L'arte organaria del rinascimento in Roma e gli organi di S. Pietro in Vaticano dalle origini a tutto il periodo Frescobaldiana.* Florence: L. S. Olschki, 1958.

Quoika, Rudolph. *Die altösterreichische Orgel der späten Gotik, der Renaissance und des Barock.* Kassel: Bärenreiter, 1953.

———. *Altösterreichische Hornwerke; eine Beltrag zur Fruhgeschichte der Orgelbaukunst.* Berlin: Merseburger, 1959.

Sumner, William Leslie. *The Organ: Its Evolution, Principles of Construction, and Use,* 3rd ed. London: Macdonald, 1962.

Williams, Peter. *The European Organ, 1450–1850.* London: Batsford, 1966.

B. *Recent Editions of Early Keyboard Music*
Compiled by G. S. Bedbrook and F. E. Kirby

Antegnati, Costanzo. *L'Antegnata. Intavolature de ricercari d'organo 1608,* Willi Apel, ed. [Dallas]: American Institute of Musicology, 1965. (*Corpus of Early Keyboard Music,* 9). Same work also ed. by S. Marega. Padua: Zanibon, 1966.

Apel, Willi, ed. *Keyboard Music of the Fourteenth and Fifteenth Centuries.* [Dallas]: American Institute of Musicology, 1963. (*Corpus of Early Keyboard Music,* 1).

Attaingnant, Pierre, ed. *Pariser Tanzbuch aus dem Jahre 1530,* 2 vols., Franz J. Giesbert, ed. Mainz: Schott, 1950.

―――. *Transcriptions of Chansons for Keyboard,* Albert Seay, ed. [Dallas]: American Institute of Musicology, 1961. (*Corpus Mensurabilis Musicae,* 20).

Auler, Wolfgang, ed. *Spielbuch für Kleinorgel oder andere Tasteninstrumente, Bd. I-II.* New York: Peters, 1951.

Benjamin Cosyn's Book. Eight Dances from Benjamin Cosyn's Second Virginal Book, Frances Cameron, ed. London: Schott, 1964.

―――. *Three Voluntaries for Organ,* John Steele, ed. London: Novello, 1959.

Fray, Juan, Bermudo. *Declaración de Instrumentos Musicales,* [facsimile] *de tañer d'organo, 1955,* Santiago Kastner, ed. Kassel: Bärenreiter, 1962.

Bull, John. *Harpsichord Pieces from Dr. John Bull's Flemish Tablature,* Hans F. Redlich, ed. Wilhelmshaven: Otto Heinrich Noetzel, 1958.

―――. *Keyboard Music,* John Steele & Francis Cameron, eds., introduction by Thurston Dart, 2 vols. London: Stainer & Bell, 1960―3. (*Musica Britannica,* 14, 19).

―――. *Ten Pieces for Keyboard,* John Steele, ed. London: Stainer & Bell, 1963.

Buus, Jacques. *Ricercari III e IV d' Intabalatura d'Organo:* Santiago Kastner, ed. Hilversum: Harmonia, 1957.

Buxheim Organ Music, Alan Booth, ed., 2 vols. London: Hinrichsen, 1959―60.

Das Buxheimer Orgelbuch [Facsimile of the manuscript] with introduction by Bertha A. Wallner. Kassel: Bärenreiter, 1955. (*Documenta musicologica,* Series II, vol. 1).

―――, modern ed. by Bertha A. Wallner, 3 vols. Kassel: Bärenreiter, 1958―9. (*Das Erbe deutscher Musik,* 37―39).

Byrd, William. *The Collected Works of William Byrd,* Edmund H. Fellowes, ed. London: Stainer & Bell, 1950. (Esp. vols. 18a, 19, 20). Revised by Thurston Dart, 1962.

―――. *Fifteen Pieces Newly Transcribed and Selected from the Fitzwilliam Virginal Book,* Thurston Dart, ed. London: Stainer & Bell, 1956.

―――. *Keyboard Music,* Alan Brown, ed. 2 vols. London: Stainer & Bell, 1969-71. (*Musica Britannica,* 27-28).

Cabezón, Antonio de. *Claviermusik; Obras de musica para tecla, arpa y vihuela,* Santiago Kastner, ed. Mainz: Schott, 1952.

166

————. *Collected Works,* Charles Jacobs, ed. Brooklyn: Institute of Mediaeval Music, 1967–. Vol. 1–.

————. *Obras de musica para tecla, arpa y vihuela,* Felipe Pedrell, ed.; revised by Higinio Anglés, 3 vols. Barcelona: 1966. (*Monumentos de la musica española, 27–29*).

————. *Pièces pour orgue,* Claude Guy, ed., 2 vols. Paris: Schola Cantorum, 1956-57). (*Orgue et Liturgie, 30–31*).

————. *Tientos und Fugen aus dem Obras . . . ,* Santiago Kastner, ed. Mainz: Schott, 1958.

Caldwell, John, ed. *Early Tudor Organ Music, I: Music for the Office.* London: Stainer & Bell, for the British Academy, 1966. (*Early English Church Music,* 6).

Cavazzoni, Girolamo. *Second Livre d'Orgue,* Jean Bonfils, ed. Paris: Schola Cantorum, 1961–. (*L'Organiste Liturgique* 34, 38).

————. *Orgelwerke,* Oscar Mischiati, ed., 2 vols. Mainz: Schott. 1959–1961. *Ricercar,* Gerald S. Bedbrook, ed. London: Schott, 1954.

————. *Ricercari, motetti, canzoni,* Giacomo Benvenuti, ed. Milan: 1941. (*I Classici Musicali Italiani,* 1).

————. *Die "Recerchari, Motetti, Canzoni, Libro Primo,"* Knud Jeppesen, ed. Copenhagen: E. Munksgaard, 1943; 2nd ed., Hansen, 1960. (*Die Italienische Orgelmusik am Anfang des Cinquecento,* 2).

Curtis, Alan, ed. *Nederlandse Klaviermuziek uit de 16e en 17e Eeuw.* Amsterdam: Vereniging voor Nederlandse Muziekgeschiedenis, 1961. (*Monumenta musica Neerlandica,* 3).

Facoli, Marco. *Collected Works,* Willi Apel, ed. [Dallas]: American Institute of Musicology, 1963. (*Corpus of Early Keyboard Music,* 2).

[Faenza Manuscript]. *An Early XV-Century Source of Keyboard Music,* [facsimile of the manuscript]. [Dallas]: American Institute of Musicology, 1961. (*Musicological Studies and Documents,* 10).

Farnaby, Gilles. *Keyboard Music,* Richard Marlow, ed. London: Stainer & Bell, 1965. (*Musica Britannica,* 24).

————. *Seventeen Pieces for Keyboard Newly Transcribed and Selected from the Fitzwilliam Virginal Book,* Thurston Dart, ed. London: Stainer & Bell, 1957.

Ferguson, Howard, ed. *Style and Interpretation: An Anthology of Keyboard Music,* 6 vols. London: Oxford University Press, 1964–71.

Fitzwilliam Virginal Book, J. A. Fuller-Maitland & William Barclay Squire, eds., 2 vols. New York: Dover, 1963. [Reprint of the London, 1899 ed.].

[————]. *Twenty-Four Pieces,* Thurston Dart, ed. London: Stainer & Bell, 1958 & 1962.

[————]. *From the Fitzwilliam Virginal Book,* M. Ettinger, ed. London: Hinrichsen, 1950.

[————]. See also William Byrd, above.

[————]. See also Giles Farnaby, above.

Frescobaldi, Girolamo, *Ausgewählte Orgelwerke in zwei Banden,* Hermann Keller, ed. Leipzig: Peters, 1943–8. Reissue, New York: Peters, 1957.

————. *Fiori Musicali, Messe della Domenica,* Charles Kope, ed. Toledo: Gregorian Institute of America, 1955.

————. *Keyboard Compositions Preserved in Manuscripts,* 3 vols. W. Richard Shindle, ed. [Dallas]: American Institute of Musicology, 1968. (*Corpus of Early Keyboard Music,* 30).

168

————, *Kyrie, Christie, Kyrie, Toccata per Elevatione*..., Norman Henne-
field, ed. New York: Liturgical Music Press, 1945.
————. *Nove Toccate Inedite,* Sandro Dalla Libera, ed. Brescia: L'Organo,
1962. (*Monumenti di Musica Italiana,* Ser. I, vol. 2).
————. *Orgel- und Klavierwerke. Gesamtausgabe nach dem Urtext,* Pierre
Pidoux, ed., 5 vols. Kassel: Bärenreiter, 1949–54.
————. *Recercari e Canzoni Franzese* [Reprint of the 1615 edition]. Farn-
borough, Hants, Eng.: Gregg, 1967.
————. *Toccate e partita d'intavolatura,* Fernando Germani, ed., 2 vols.
Rome: De Santis, 1936–7. Reissue, 1951.
Gabrieli, Andrea. *Canzonen und Ricercari ariosi für Orgel,* Pierre Pidoux,
ed. Kassel: Bärenreiter, 1953.
————. *Canzoni alla francese für Orgel oder Cembalo,* Pierre Pidoux, ed.
Kassel: Bärenrieter, 1953.
————. *Intonationen für Orgel,* Pierre Pidoux, ed. Bärenreiter, 1959.
————. *Ricercari für Orgel,* Pierre Pidoux, ed. 2 vols. Kassel: Bärenreiter,
1953–9.
————. *3 Messe per organo,* Sandro Dalla Libera, ed. Milan: Ricordi, 1959.
————. *Toccate per organo,* Sandro Dalla Libera, ed. Milan: Ricordi, 1961.
————. *Toccate,* Ernest White, ed. New York: Liturgical Music Press, 1952.
Gabrieli, Giovanni. *Composizioni per Organo,* Sandro Dalla Libera, ed., 3
vols. Milan: Ricordi, 1957–9.
————. *Opera omnia,* Denis Arnold, ed. [Dallas]: American Institute of
Musicology. (*Corpus Mensurabilis Musicae,* 12). [Keyboard music has
yet to appear].
————. *Werke für Tastinstrumente,* Gerald S. Bedbrook, ed. Kassel:
Bärenreiter, 1957.
Gibbons, Orlando. *Keyboard Music,* Gerald Hendrie. ed. London: Stainer &
Bell, 1962. (*Musica Britannica,* 20).
Golos, Jerzy and Adam Sutkowski, eds. *Keyboard Music from Polish Manu-
scripts* [4 vols. to date]. [Dallas]: American Institute of Musicology,
1965–. (*Corpus of Early Keyboard Music,* 10).
Hassler, Hans Leo. *Ricercari, Canzoni & Ricercar,* Norman Hennefield, ed.
New York: Liturgical Music Press, 1956.
————. *Sämtliche Werke,* C. Russell Crosby, Jr., ed. Wiesbaden: Breitkopf
& Härtel, 1961–. (*Veröffentlichungen der Gesellschaft für Bayerische
Musik-Geschichte*). [Keyboard music has yet to appear].
Heartz, Daniel, ed. *Keyboard Dances from the Earlier 16th Century.* [Dallas]:
American Institute of Musicology, 1965. (*Corpus of Early Keyboard
Music,* 8).
Henry VIII. *Three Songs,* A. Gaylord, ed. London: Coptic Press, 1966.
[Hofhaimer, Paul]. *Hofhaimers Gesammelten Tonwerken* [*i.e.,* 91 Ton-
sätze P. Hofhaimers und seines Krises*], Hans Joachim Moser, ed., in his
Paul Hofhaimer. Stuttgart: J. C. Cotta, 1929; reprint, 1967.
————. *Salve Regina,* [Completed by Hans Kotter] Denis Stevens, ed.
London: Hinrichsen, 1960.
Ileborgh, Adam. *Die Orgeltabulatur* [facsimile reproduction of the manu-
script]. Altmärkische Museum, *Jahresausgabe* VII (Stendal: 1954),
43–66.

————. *Die Orgeltabulatur,* Willi Apel, ed. [Dallas]: American Institute of Musicology, 1963. (*Corpus of Early Keyboard Music,* 1).

Intabolatura nova di balli (Venice, 1551), William Oxenbury and Thurston Dart, eds. London: Stainer & Bell, 1965.

Jackson, Roland, ed. *Neapolitan Keyboard Compositions (circa 1600).* [Dallas]: American Institute of Musicology, 1967. (*Corpus of Early Keyboard Music,* 23).

Jeppesen, Knud, ed. *Balli Antichi Veneziani per Cembalo.* Copenhagen: Hansen, 1962.

[Kotter, Hans]. *Die Tabulaturen aus dem Besitz des Basler Humanisten Bonifacius Amerbach,* Hans Joachim Marx, ed. Kassel: Bärenreiter, 1967. (*Schweizerische Musikdenkmäler,* 6).

Kraus, Eberhard, ed. *Altenglische Orgelmusik.* Regensburg: Pustet, 1968.

Lublin, Johannes de. *Tablature of Keyboard Music,* John Reeves White, ed., 6 vols. [Dallas]: American Institute of Musicology, 1964–. (*Corpus of Early Keyboard Music,* 6).

Marr, Peter, ed. *Early German Organ Music.* London: Hinrichsen, 1967.

Merulo, Claudio. *Canzonen 1592, für Orgel und andere Tasteninstrumente,* Pierre Pidoux, ed. Kassel: Bärenreiter, 1954.

————. *Four Toccatas,* Gerald S. Bedbrook, ed. London: Schott, 1954.

————. *Toccate per organo,* Sandro Dalla Libera, ed. 3 vols. Milan: Ricordi, 1959–60.

————. *Composizione per Organo.* Alan Curtis, ed. Kassel: Bärenreiter, 1961.

Morley, Thomas. *Keyboard Works.* Thurston Dart, ed., 2 vols. London: Stainer & Bell, 1959.

Mulliner Book, Denis Stevens, ed. London: Stainer & Bell, 1951; revised ed., 1954. (*Musica Britannica,* 1).

[————]. *Altenglische Klaviermusik aus dem Mulliner Buch,* Denis Stevens ed. Kassel: Bärenreiter, 1953.

————. *Altenglische Orgelmusik,* Denis Stevens, ed. Kassel: Bärenreiter, 1954.

————. *Orgelmusik aus dem Mulliner Buch,* Hans Redlich, ed. Wilhelmshaven: Otto Heinrich Noetzel, 1958.

————. *Twelve Pieces from Mulliner's Book* (ca. 1555), Frank Dawes, ed. London: Schott, 1951. (*Schott's Anthology of Early Music,* 3).

[————]. See also Thomas Tallis, below.

Padovano, Annibale. *Composizioni per Organo.* Fiorella Benetti, ed. Padova Zanibon, 1962.

Parthenia, [Reprint], with introduction by Otto Erich Deutsch. Cambridge: Heffer, 1942. (*The Harrow Replicas,* 3).

————. [Reprint]. New York: Broude Bros., 1967. (*Monuments of Music and Music Literature in Facsimile,* Ser. I, Vol. 11).

————, modern edition by Kurt Stone. New York: Broude, 1951.

————, Thurston Dart, ed. London: Stainer & Bell, 1962.

Peeters, Flor, ed. *Alte Orgelmusik aus England und Frankreich.* Mainz: Schott, 1958.

————, ed. *Altniederländische Meister für Orgel oder Harmonium.* Mainz: Schott, 1958.

Radino, Giovanni M. *Il Primo libro d'intavolatura di balli d'arpicordo* [Facsimile of 1592 ed.]. Rosamond Harding, ed. Cambridge: W. Heffer, 1949.

Sancta Maria, Tomas de. *Oeuvres transcrites de l'Arte tañer Fantasie,* Pierre Froidebise, ed. Paris: Schola Cantorum, 1961—62.

Scheidt, Samuel, *Alanado. 10 Variations for Harpsichord,* Oscar Mischiate, ed. London: Schott, 1967.

———. *Ausgewählte Werke,* Hermann Keller, ed. New York: Peters, 1939, reissued as *Samuel Scheidt Album,* London: Peters, 1957.

———. *6 Choral Preludes (on "When Jesus was on the Cross"),* Walter Buszin, ed. St. Louis: Concordia Publishing House, 1954.

———. *Das Görlitzer Tabulaturbuch aus dem Jahre 1650,* Fritz Dietrich, ed. Kassel: Bärenreiter, 1954.

———. *Das Görlitzer Tabulaturbuch vom Jahre 1650,* Christhard Mahrenholz, ed. Leipzig: Peters, 1941; reissue, New York: Peters, 1955.

———. *Magnificat (on the 9th tone). "When Jesus on the Cross was found,"* Norman Hennefield, ed. New York: Liturgical Music Press, 1944.

———. *Werke,* Gottlieb Harms and Christhard Mahrenholz, eds. Hamburg: Ugrino Verlag, 1923—.
I. *Tabulatur-Buch vom Jahre 1650.* (1923)
II/III. *Paduana, Galliarda, Couranta, Alemande, Intrada, Canzonetto.* (1928)
V. *Unedierte kompositionen fur Tasteninstrumente* (1937).
VI. *Tabulatura nova, Teil I und II* (1953).
VII. *Tabulatura nova, Teil III* (1953).

Schering, Arnold, ed. *Alte Meister aus der Frühzeit des Orgelspiels.* Leipzig: Breitkopf & Härtel, 1913; reissue, 1964.

[Schlick, Arnoldt]. *Hommage à l'Empereur Charles Quint,* Santiago Kastner and M. Querol Gavaldá, eds. Barcelona: Borleau, 1954.

———. *Tabulaturen,* Gottlieb Harms, ed. Klecken: Ugrino, 1924; reissue, Hamburg: Urgino, 1957.

———. *Tabulaturen,* Norman Hennefield, ed. New York: Liturgical Music Press, 1947.

Schmidt, Jost Harro, ed. *Orgelmusik der Reformationszeit. Orgelmeister der Renaissance.* Berlin: Verlag Merseburger, 1965.

[Sicher, Fridolin]. *Ein altes Spielbuch aus der Zeit um 1500,* Franz Julius Giesbert, ed., 2 vols. Mainz: Schott, 1936.

Sweelinck, Jan Pietersz. *Ausgewählte Werke für Orgel und Klavier,* Diethard Hellmann, ed., 2 vols. New York: Peters, 1957.

———. *Choralbearbeitungen, Deutsche Erstveröffentlichung aus der Tabulatur Lynar A—1,* Hans Joachim Moser and Traugott Fedtke, eds. Kassel: Bärenreiter, 1965.

———. *Fantasia (Ionish) Bureau vor Nederlandse Orgelkunst,* Jan Swart, Jr., ed. Rotterdam: [n. d.].

———. *Variationen auf "Mein junges Leben hat ein End."* Karl Straube, ed. London: Hinrichsen, 1956.

———. *O Mensch bewein dein Sünde Gross. Choralpartita für Orgel.* Mainz: Schott, 1967.

———. *Opera Omnia,* 10 vols. Amsterdam · Alsbach, 1967—.

———. *Opera Organis Concinenda,* Adriaan Engles, ed. The Hague: Editio Musico, 1959—. (*Musica Antiqua Batava*).

——. *Three Chorale Variations,* Flor Peeters, ed. New York: Peters, 1965.

——. *Werke für Orgel und Klavier,* Flor Peeters, ed., 3 vols.

——. *Werken van Jan Pieterszon Sweelinck,* Max Seiffert, ed. Amsterdam: G. Alsbach, 1943–.

I. *Werken voor Orgel en Clavecimbel,* Max Seiffert, ed. (1943)

I., Supplement. *Werken voor Orgel en Clavecimbel,* Alfons Annegarn, ed. (1958)

——. *Werken voor Orgel of Clavecimbel uit het "Celler Klavierbuch 1962,"* Jost Harro Schmidt, ed. Amsterdam: Vereniging voor Nederlandse Muziekgeschiedenis, 1965. (*Exempla musica Neerlandica,* 2).

Tallis, Thomas. *Complete Keyboard Works,* Denis Stevens, ed. London: Hinrichsen, 1953. 2nd ed., 1962.

——. *3 Organ Hymn Verses and 4 Antiphons,* Denis Stevens, ed., London: Hinrichsen, 1953.

——. *4 Pieces partly from the Mulliner Book,* Denis Stevens, ed. London: Hinrichsen, 1953.

Tisdale's Virginal Book, Alan Brown, ed. London: Stainer & Bell, 1966.

Titelouze, Jean *Hymnes de l'église pour toucher l'orgue,* Norbert Dufourcq, ed. Paris: Bornemann, 1965.

——. *Pange Lingue Glorisosi, the Passion Hymn for Organ,* William L. Sumner, ed. New York: Peters, 1957.

Trabaci, Giovanni Maria. *Composizioni per organo e cembalo,* Oscar Mischiati, ed. Brescia: L'Organo, 1964. (*Monumenti di musica Italiana,* Ser. I, Vol. 3).

Valente, Antonio. *43 Versi spirituali,* Ireneo Fuser, ed. Padua: G. Zanibon, 1958.

Valentin, Erich, ed. *The Toccata.* Cologne: Arno Volk, 1958. (*Anthology of Music,* 17). German edition as *Die Tokkata* (*Das Musikwerk,* 17).

Venegas de Henestrosa, Luis. *Libro di cifra nueva* (*Alcala de Henares, 1557*), Higinio Anglés, ed. Barcelona: Instituto español de musicología, 1944. (Monumentos de la musica española, 2).